Undergraduate Topics in Computer Science

Undergraduate Topics in Computer Science (UTiCS) delivers high-quality instructional content for undergraduates studying in all areas of computing and information science. From core foundational and theoretical material to final-year topics and applications, UTiCS books take a fresh, concise, and modern approach and are ideal for self-study or for a one- or two-semester course. The texts are all authored by established experts in their fields, reviewed by an international advisory board, and contain numerous examples and problems. Many include fully worked solutions.

For other volumes:
http://www.springer.com/series/7592

Gilles Dowek · Jean-Jacques Lévy

Introduction
to the Theory
of Programming
Languages

 Springer

Gilles Dowek
Labo. d'Informatique
École polytechnique
route de Saclay
91128 Palaiseau
France
gilles.dowek@polytechnique.edu

Jean-Jacques Lévy
Centre de Recherche Commun
INRIA-Microsoft Research
Parc Orsay Université
28 rue Jean Rostand
91893 Orsay Cedex
France
jean-jacques.levy@inria.fr

The work was first published in 2006 by Les editions de l'École polytechnique with the following title: 'Introduction à la théorie des langages de programmation'. The translator of the work is Maribel Fernandez.

ISSN 1863-7310
ISBN 978-0-85729-075-5   e-ISBN 978-0-85729-076-2
DOI 10.1007/978-0-85729-076-2
Springer London Dordrecht Heidelberg New York

British Library Cataloguing in Publication Data
A catalogue record for this book is available from the British Library

What Is the Theory of Programming Languages?

The ultimate, definitive programming language has not been created yet, far from it. Almost every day a new language is created, and new functionalities are added to existing languages. Improvements in programming languages contribute to making programs more reliable, shorten the development time, and make programs easier to maintain. Improvements are also needed to satisfy new requirements, such as the development of parallel, distributed or mobile programs.

The first thing that we need to describe, when defining a programming language, is its *syntax*. Should we write x := 1 or x = 1? Should we put brackets after an if or not? More generally, what are the strings of symbols that can be used as a program? There is a useful tool for this: the notion of a *formal grammar*. Using a grammar, we can describe the syntax of the language in a precise way, and this makes it possible to build programs to check the syntactical correctness of programs.

But it is not sufficient to know what a syntactically correct program is in order to know what is going to happen when we run the program. When defining a programming language, it is also necessary to describe its *semantics*, that is, the expected behaviour of the program when it is executed. Two languages may have the same syntax but different semantics.

The following is an example of what is meant (informally) by semantics. Function evaluation is often explained as follows. *"The result* V *of the evaluation of an expression of the form* f e_1 ... e_n, *where the symbol* f *is a function defined by the expression* f x_1 ... x_n = e', *is obtained in the following way. First, the arguments* e_1, ..., e_n *are evaluated, returning values* W_1, ..., W_n. *Then, these values are associated to the variables* x_1, ..., x_n, *and finally the expression* e' *is evaluated. The value* V *is the result of this evaluation."*

This explanation of the semantics of the language, expressed in a natural language (English), allows us to understand what happens when a program is executed, but is it precise? Consider, for example, the program

```
f x y = x
g z = (n = n + z; n)
n = 0; print(f (g 2) (g 7))
```

Depending on the way we interpret the explanation given above, we can deduce that the program will result in the value 2 or in the value 9. This is because the natural language explanation does not indicate whether we have to evaluate $g\ 2$ before or after $g\ 7$, and the order in which we evaluate these expressions is important in this case. Instead, the explanation should have said: "the arguments $e_1, \ldots, e_n$ are evaluated *starting from* e_1" or else "*starting from* e_n".

If two different programmers read an ambiguous explanation, they might understand different things. Even worse, the designers of the compilers for the language might choose different conventions. Then the same program will give different results depending on the compiler used.

It is well known that natural languages are too imprecise to express the syntax of a programming language, a formal language should be used instead. Similarly, natural languages are too imprecise to express the semantics of a programming language, and we need to use a formal language for this.

What is the semantics of a program? Let us take for instance a program p that requests an integer, computes its square, and displays the result of this operation. To describe the behaviour of this program, we need to describe a relation R between the input value and the associated output.

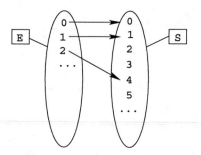

The semantics of this program is, thus, a relation R between elements of the set E of input values and elements of the set S of output values, that is, a subset of $E \times S$.

The semantics of a program is then a binary relation. The semantics of a programming language is, in turn, a ternary relation: "the program p with input value e returns the output value s". We denote this relation by $p,\ e \hookrightarrow s$. The program p and the input e are available before the execution of the program starts. Often, these two elements are paired in a *term* $p\ e$, and the semantics of the language assigns a value to this term. The semantics of the language is then a binary relation $t \hookrightarrow s$.

To express the semantics of a programming language we need a language that can express relations.

When the semantics of a program is a functional relation, that is, for each input value there is at most one output value, we say that the program is *deterministic*. Video games are examples of non-deterministic programs, since some randomness is necessary to make the game enjoyable. A language is deterministic if all the programs that can be written in the language are deterministic, or equivalently, if the semantics is a functional relation. In this case, it is possible to define its semantics using a language to define functions instead of a language to define relations.

Acknowledgements

The authors would like to thank Gérard Assayag, Antonio Bucciarelli, Roberto Di Cosmo, Xavier Leroy, Dave MacQueen, Luc Maranget, Michel Mauny, François Pottier, Didier Rémy, Alan Schmitt, Élodie-Jane Sims and Véronique Viguié Donzeau-Gouge.

Contents

Chapter 1
Terms and Relations

1.1 Inductive Definitions

Since the semantics of a programming language is a relation, we will start by introducing some tools to define sets and relations.

The most basic tool is the notion of an *explicit definition*. We can, for example, define explicitly the function that multiplies its argument by 2: $x \mapsto 2 * x$, the set of even numbers: $\{n \in \mathbb{N} \mid \exists p \in \mathbb{N} \; n = 2 * p\}$, or the divisibility relation: $\{(n,m) \in \mathbb{N}^2 \mid \exists p \in \mathbb{N} \; n = m * p\}$. However, these explicit definitions are not sufficient to define all the objects we need. A second tool to define sets and relations is the notion of an *inductive definition*. This notion is based on a simple theorem: the fixed point theorem.

1.1.1 The Fixed Point Theorem

Let $\leq$ be an ordering relation—that is, a reflexive, antisymmetric and transitive relation—over a set E, and let u_0, u_1, u_2, ... be an increasing sequence, that is, a sequence such that $u_0 \leq u_1 \leq u_2 \leq \; \ldots$ The element l of E is called *limit* of the sequence u_0, u_1, u_2, ... if it is a least upper bound of the set $\{u_0, u_1, u_2, \ldots\}$, that is, if

- for all i, $u_i \leq l$
- if, for all i, $u_i \leq l'$, then $l \leq l'$.

If it exists, the limit of a sequence $(u_i)_i$ is unique, and we denote it by $\lim_i u_i$.

The ordering relation $\leq$ is said to be *weakly complete* if all the increasing sequences have a limit.

The standard ordering relation over the real numbers interval $[0, 1]$ is an example of a weakly complete ordering. In addition, this relation has a least element 0. However, the standard ordering relation over $\mathbb{R}^+$ is not weakly complete since the increasing sequence 0, 1, 2, 3, ... does not have a limit.

G. Dowek, J.-J. Lévy, *Introduction to the Theory of Programming Languages*,
Undergraduate Topics in Computer Science,
DOI 10.1007/978-0-85729-076-2_1, © Springer-Verlag London Limited 2011

Let A be an arbitrary set. The inclusion relation $\subseteq$ over the set $\wp(A)$ of all the subsets of A is another example of a weakly complete ordering. The limit of an increasing sequence U_0, U_1, U_2, ... is the set $\bigcup_{i \in \mathbb{N}} U_i$. In addition, this relation has a least element $\varnothing$.

Let f be a function from E to E. The function f is *increasing* if

$$x \le y \implies f\ x \le f\ y.$$

It is *continuous* if, in addition, for any increasing sequence

$$\lim_i (f\ u_i) = f\ (\lim_i u_i).$$

First Fixed Point Theorem *Let $\le$ be a weakly complete ordering relation over a set E that has a least element m. Let f be a function from E to E. If f is continuous then $p = \lim_i\ (f^i\ m)$ is the least fixed point of f.*

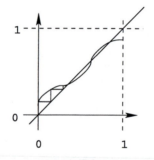

Proof First, since m is the smallest element in E, $m \le f\ m$. The function f is increasing, therefore $f^i\ m \le f^{i+1}\ m$. Since the sequence $f^i\ m$ is increasing, it has a limit. The sequence $f^{i+1}\ m$ also has p as limit, thus, $p = \lim_i\ (f\ (f^i\ m)) = f\ (\lim_i\ (f^i\ m)) = f\ p$. Moreover, p is the least fixed point, because if q is another fixed point, then $m \le q$ and $f^i\ m \le f^i\ q = q$ (since f is increasing). Hence $p = \lim_i\ (f^i\ m) \le q$.

The second fixed point theorem states the existence of a fixed point for increasing functions, even if they are not continuous, provided the ordering satisfies a stronger property.

An ordering $\le$ over a set E is *strongly complete* if every subset A of E has a least upper bound sup A.

The standard ordering relation over the interval $[0, 1]$ is an example of a strongly complete ordering relation. The standard ordering over $\mathbb{R}^+$ is not strongly complete because the set $\mathbb{R}^+$ itself has no upper bound.

Let A be an arbitrary set. The inclusion relation $\subseteq$ over the set $\wp(A)$ of all the subsets of A is another example of strongly complete ordering. The least upper bound of a set B is the set $\bigcup_{C \in B} C$. ☐

Exercise 1.1 Show that any strongly complete ordering is also weakly complete. Is the ordering weakly complete? Is it strongly complete?

Note that if the ordering $\leq$ over the set E is strongly complete, then any subset A of E has a greatest lower bound $\inf$ A. Indeed, let A be a subset of E, let B be the set $\{y \in E \mid \forall x \in A\ y \leq x\}$ of lower bounds of A and 1 the least upper bound of B. By definition, 1 is an upper bound of the set B

$- \forall y \in B\ y \leq 1$

and it is the least one

$- (\forall y \in B\ y \leq 1') \Rightarrow 1 \leq 1'$

It is easy to show that 1 is the greatest lower bound of A. Indeed, if x is an element of A, it is an upper bound of B and since 1 is the least upper bound, $1 \leq x$. Thus, 1 is a lower bound of A. To show that it is the greatest one, it is sufficient to note that if m is another lower bound of A, it is an element of B and therefore $m \leq 1$.

The greatest lower bound of a set B of subsets of A is, of course, the set $\bigcap_{C \in B} C$.

Second Fixed Point Theorem *Let $\leq$ be a strongly complete ordering over a set E. Let f be a function from E to E. If f is increasing then* $p = \inf\ \{c \mid f\ c \leq c\}$ *is the least fixed point of* f.

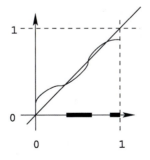

Proof Let C be the set $\{c \mid f\ c \leq c\}$ and c be an element of C. Then $p \leq c$ because p is a lower bound of C. Since the function f is increasing, we deduce

that f p ≤ f c. Also, f c ≤ c because c is an element of C, so by transitivity
f p ≤ c.

The element f p is smaller than all the elements in C, it is therefore also smaller
than or equal to its greatest lower bound: f p ≤ p.

Since the function f is increasing, f (f p) ≤ f p, thus f p is an element
of C, and since p is a lower bound of C, we deduce p ≤ f p. By antisymmetry,
p = f p.

Finally, by definition, all the fixed points of f belong to C, and they are therefore
greater than p.   □

1.1.2 Inductive Definitions

We will now see how these fixed point theorems can be used to define sets and
relations.

Let A be a set, f a function from A^n to A and E a subset of A. The set E is *closed*
under the function f if for all a_1, ..., a_n in E, f a_1 ... a_n is also in E. For
example, the set of all the even numbers is closed under the function $n \mapsto n + 2$.

Let A be a set. An *inductive definition* of a subset E of A is a family of partial
functions f_1 from A^{n_1} to A, f_2 from A^{n_2} to A, ... The set E is defined as the
smallest subset of A that is closed under the functions f_1, f_2, ...

For example, the subset of $\mathbb{N}$ that contains all the even numbers is inductively
defined by the number 0—that is, the function from $\mathbb{N}^0$ to $\mathbb{N}$ that returns the value
0—and the function from $\mathbb{N}$ to $\mathbb{N}$ $n \mapsto n + 2$. The subset of $\{a, b, c\}^*$ containing all the words of the form $a^n b c^n$ is inductively defined by the word b and the
function $m \mapsto a\ m\ c$. In general, a context free grammar can always be specified
as an inductive set. In logic, the set of theorems is defined as the subset of all the
propositions that is inductively defined by the axioms and deduction rules.

The functions f_1, f_2, ... are called *rules*. Instead of writing a rule as
x_1 ... $x_n \mapsto t$, we will use the notation

$$\frac{x_1 \ \ldots \ x_n}{t}$$

For example, the set of even numbers is defined by the rules

$$\frac{}{0}$$

$$\frac{n}{n + 2}$$

Let P be the set of even numbers. We will sometimes write the rules as follows:

$$\frac{}{0 \in P}$$

$$\frac{n \in P}{n + 2 \in P}$$

In order to define a language inductively, we will sometimes use a notation borrowed from language theory, where, for example, the set of words of the form $a^n b c^n$ is defined as follows

$m = b$
$\quad | \; a \; m \; c$

To show that there is indeed a smallest subset of A that is closed under the functions f_1, f_2, ..., we define a function F from $\wp(A)$ to $\wp(A)$

$$F \; C = \{x \in A \mid \exists i \; \exists y_1 \ldots y_{n_i} \in C \; x = f_i \; y_1 \; \ldots \; y_{n_i}\}$$

A subset C of A is closed under the functions f_1, f_2, ... if and only if $F \; C \subseteq C$.

The function F is trivially increasing, that is, if $C \subseteq C'$ then $F \; C \subseteq F \; C'$. In addition, it is continuous, that is, if $C_0 \subseteq C_1 \subseteq C_2 \subseteq \cdots$ then $F \; (\bigcup_j C_j) = \bigcup_j (F \; C_j)$. Indeed, if an element x of A is in $F \; (\bigcup_j C_j)$, then there exists a number i and elements y_1, ..., y_{n_i} in $\bigcup_j C_j$ such that $x = f_i \; y_1 \; \ldots \; y_{n_i}$. Each of these elements is in one of the C_j. Since the sequence C_j is increasing, they are all in C_k, which is the largest of these sets. Therefore, the element x belongs to $F \; C_k$ and also to $\bigcup_j (F \; C_j)$. Conversely, if x is in $\bigcup_j (F \; C_j)$, then it belongs to some $F \; C_k$, and there is therefore a number i and elements y_1, ..., y_{n_i} of C_k such that $x = f_i \; y_1 \; \ldots \; y_{n_i}$. The elements y_1, ..., y_{n_i} are in $\bigcup_j C_j$, and therefore x is in $F \; (\bigcup_j C_j)$.

The set E is defined as the least fixed point of the function F. This is the smallest set that satisfies the property $F \; E = E$ and, according to the second fixed point theorem, it is also the smallest set that satisfies the property $F \; E \subseteq E$. Thus, it is the smallest set that is closed under the functions f_1, f_2, ...

The set of even numbers is not the only subset of $\mathbb{N}$ that contains 0 and is closed under the function $n \mapsto n + 2$—the set $\mathbb{N}$, for example, also satisfies these properties—but it is the smallest one. It can be defined as the intersection of all those sets. The second fixed point theorem allows us to generalise this observation and define E as the intersection of all the sets that are closed under the functions f_1, f_2, ...

The first fixed point theorem shows that an element x is in E if and only if there is some number k such that x is in the set $F^k \; \varnothing$. That is, if there is a function f_i such that $x = f_i \; y_1 \; \ldots \; y_{n_i}$ where y_1, ..., y_{n_i} are in $F^{k-1} \; \varnothing$. Iterating, that is, by induction on k, we can show that an element x of A is in E if and only if there exists a tree where the nodes are labelled by elements of A, the root is labelled by x, and if a node is labelled by c, then its children are labelled by d_1, ..., d_n such that for some rule f, we have $c = f \; d_1 \; \ldots \; d_n$. Such a tree is called a *derivation* for a. This notion of a derivation generalises the notion of proof in logic. We can then define the set E as the set of elements x of A for which there is a derivation.

We will use a specific notation for derivations. First, the root of the tree will be written at the bottom, and the leaves at the top. Then, we will write a line over each node in the tree and we will write its children over the line.

The number 8, for example, is in the set of even numbers, as the following derivation shows

$$\cfrac{\cfrac{\cfrac{\cfrac{\cfrac{0}{2}}{4}}{6}}{8}}{}$$

If we call P the set of even numbers, we can write the derivation as follows

$$\cfrac{\cfrac{\cfrac{\cfrac{\cfrac{0 \in P}{2 \in P}}{4 \in P}}{6 \in P}}{8 \in P}}{}$$

1.1.3 Structural Induction

Inductive definitions suggest a method to write proofs. If a property is hereditary, that is, if each time it holds for $y_1, \ldots, y_{n_i}$, then it also holds for $f_i \; y_1 \ldots y_{n_i}$, then we can deduce that it holds for all the elements of E.

One way to show this, is to use the second fixed point theorem and to observe that the subset P of A containing all the elements that satisfy the property is closed under the functions f_i and thus it includes E. Another way is to use the first fixed point theorem and to show by induction on k that all the elements in $F^k \; \varnothing$ satisfy the property.

1.1.4 The Reflexive-Transitive Closure of a Relation

The reflexive-transitive closure of a relation is an example of inductive definition. If R is a binary relation on a set A, we can inductively define another relation R*, called the reflexive-transitive closure of R

$$\frac{}{x \; R^* \; y} \; \text{if } x \; R \; y$$

$$\frac{}{x \; R^* \; x}$$

$$\frac{x \; R^* \; y \quad y \; R^* \; z}{x \; R^* \; z}$$

If we see R as a directed graph, then R* is the relation that links two nodes when there is a path from one to the other.

1.2 Languages

1.2.1 Languages Without Variables

Now that we have introduced inductive definitions, we will use this technique to define the notion of a *language*. The notion of language that we will define does not take into account superficial syntactic conventions, for instance, it does not matter whether we write 3 + 4, +(3,4), or 3 4 +. This term will be represented in an abstract way by a tree. Each node in the tree will be labelled by a symbol. The

number of children of a node depends on the node's label—2 children if the label is +, 0 if it is 3 or 4, ...

A language is thus a set of symbols, each with an associated number called *arity*, or simply *number of arguments*, of the symbol. The symbols without arguments are called *constants*.

The set of *terms* of the language is the set of trees inductively defined by

– if f is a symbol with n arguments and t_1, ..., t_n are terms then $f(t_1, ..., t_n)$—that is, the tree that has a root labelled by f and subtrees t_1, ..., t_n—is a term.

1.2.2 Variables

Imagine that we want to design a language to define functions. One possibility would be to use constants sin, cos, ... and a symbol with two arguments o. We could, for instance, build the term sin o (cos o sin) in this language.

However, we know that, to specify functions, it is easier to use a notion invented by F. Viète (1540–1603): the notion of a variable. Thus, the function described above can be written sin (cos (sin x)).

Since the 1930's, we write this function x ↦ sin (cos (sin x)) or λx sin (cos (sin x)), using the symbol ↦ or λ to *bind* the variable x. By indicating explicitly which variables are bound, we can distinguish the arguments of the function from potential parameters, and we also fix the order of the arguments.

The symbol $\mapsto$ appears to have been introduced by N. Bourbaki around 1930, and the symbol λ by A. Church around the same time. The notation λ is a simplified version of a previous notation $\hat{x}$ `sin (cos (sin x))` used by A.N. Whitehead and B. Russell since the 1900's.

The definition `f = x` $\mapsto$ `sin (cos (sin x))` is sometimes written `f x = sin (cos (sin x))`. The advantage of writing `f = x` $\mapsto$ `sin (cos (sin x))` is that in this way we can distinguish two different operations: the *construction* of the function `x` $\mapsto$ `sin (cos (sin x))` and the *definition* itself, which gives a name to an object previously constructed. It is often important, in computer science, to have notations that allow us to build objects without necessarily giving them a name.

In this book, we use the notation `fun x -> sin (cos (sin x))` to specify this function.

The term `fun x -> sin (cos (sin x))` specifies a function. However, its subterm `sin x` does not specify anything: it is not a real number and it is not a function, because it contains a *free variable* whose value we do not know.

To bind variables in terms, we need to extend the notion of term to include free variables, which will be bound later. This requires also new symbols, such as `fun`, which act as binders for the variables in some of their arguments. Other examples of binders are the symbol $\{\ \ |\ \ \}$, the symbol ∂/∂, the symbol $\int d$, the symbols $\sum$ and $\prod$, the quantifiers $\forall$ and $\exists$, ... In this book we will use several binders: the symbol `fun` above, the symbols `fix`, `let`, `fixfun` ....

The arity of a symbol f will no longer be a number n, instead, we will use a finite sequence of numbers $(k_1, \ldots, k_n)$ that will indicate that f binds k_1 variables in its first argument, k_2 variables in the second, ..., k_n variables in the nth.

In this way, when a language is defined—that is, a set of symbols with their arities—and an infinite set of *variables* is given, we can define the set of terms inductively as follows

- variables are terms,
- if f is a symbol with arity $(k_1, \ldots, k_n)$, $t_1, \ldots, t_n$ are terms and $x_1^1, \ldots, x_{k_1}^1, \ldots, x_1^n, \ldots, x_{k_n}^n$ are variables, then $f(x_1^1 \ldots x_{k_1}^1 t_1, \ldots, x_1^n \ldots x_{k_n}^n t_n)$ is a term.

The notation $f(x_1^1 \ldots x_{k_1}^1 t_1, \ldots, x_1^n \ldots x_{k_n}^n t_n)$ denotes the tree

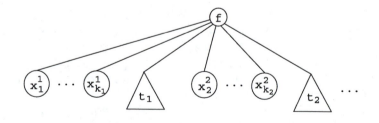

This definition can be better understood with an example. We build a language in which terms specify real numbers and functions over the reals, and which includes

two constants `sin` and `cos` to represent the functions sine and cosine, a symbol α, called *application*, such that α (`f,x`) is the object obtained by applying the function `f` to the object `x` and a symbol `fun` to build functions. This language includes then four symbols: the constants `sin` and `cos`, α with arity (`0,0`) and `fun` with arity (`1`); the set of terms is inductively defined by

- variables are terms,
- `sin` is a term,
- `cos` is a term,
- if `t` and `u` are terms then α (`t,u`) is a term,
- if `t` is a term and `x` is a variable then `fun(x t)` is a term.

We will adopt a simplified notation, writing `t u` for the term α (`t,u`) and `fun x -> t` for the term `fun(x t)`.

For example, `fun x -> sin (cos (sin x))` is a term in this language.

1.2.3 Many-Sorted Languages

In this book, we will sometimes use more general languages, called *many-sorted languages*. For instance, the language that is used to describe vectors with a finite number of constants, addition and scalar multiplication. In this language, there are two sorts of terms: terms describing a vector, and terms describing a scalar. In the definition of the language we indicate that the symbol + has two arguments, *that are both vectors* and that the symbol . has two arguments, *which are a scalar and a vector*.

For this, we introduce a set with two elements {`vect, scal`}, called *sorts*, and we associate to the symbol . the arity (`scal, vect, vect`). This arity indicates that in a term of the form $\lambda . v$, the term λ must be of sort `scal`, the term v of sort `vect`, and the term $\lambda . v$ is itself of sort `vect`.

When, in addition, there are bound variables, the arity of a symbol `f` is a finite sequence $((s_1^1, \ldots, s_{k_1}^1, s'^1), \ldots, (s_1^n, \ldots, s_{k_n}^n, s'^n), s'')$ indicating that the symbol has n arguments, the first one of sort s'_1 and binding k_1 variables of sorts $s_1^1, \ldots, s_{k_1}^1, \ldots$, and that the resulting term is itself of sort s''.

Given a language—that is, a set of sorts and a set of symbols each with an associated arity—and a family, indexed by sorts, of infinite, pairwise disjoint, sets of variables, we can inductively define terms as follows:

- variables of sort s are terms of sort s,
- if `f` is a symbol of arity $((s_1^1, \ldots, s_{k_1}^1, s'^1), \ldots, (s_1^n, \ldots, s_{k_n}^n, s'^n), s''), x_1^1, \ldots, x_{k_1}^1, \ldots, x_1^n, \ldots, x_{k_n}^n$ are variables of sort $s_1^1, \ldots, s_{k_1}^1, \ldots, s_1^n, \ldots, s_{k_n}^n$ and $t_1, \ldots, t_n$ are terms of sort $s'^1, \ldots, s'^n$ then $f(x_1^1 \ldots x_{k_1}^1 t_1, \ldots, x_1^n \ldots x_{k_n}^n t_n)$ is a term of sort s''.

1.2.4 Free and Bound Variables

The set of variables of a term is defined by structural induction:

- $\text{Var}(x) = \{x\}$,
- $\text{Var}(f(x_1^1 \ \ldots \ x_{k_1}^1 \ t_1, \ \ldots, \ x_1^n \ \ldots \ x_{k_n}^n \ t_n)) = \text{Var}(t_1) \ \cup \ \{x_1^1, \ \ldots, \ x_{k_1}^1\} \ \cup \cdots \cup \ \text{Var}(t_n) \ \cup \ \{x_n^n, \ \ldots, \ x_{k_n}^n\}$.

We can also define the set of free variables of a term:

- $\text{FV}(x) = \{x\}$,
- $\text{FV}(f(x_1^1 \ \ldots \ x_{k_1}^1 \ t_1, \ \ldots, \ x_1^n \ \ldots \ x_{k_n}^n \ t_n)) = (\text{FV}(t_1) \ \backslash \ \{x_1^1, \ \ldots, \ x_{k_1}^1\}) \ \cup \cdots \cup \ (\text{FV}(t_n) \ \backslash \ \{x_n^n, \ \ldots, \ x_{k_n}^n\})$

For example, Var (fun x -> sin (cos (sin x))) $= \{x\}$ and FV (fun x -> sin (cos (sin x))) $= \emptyset$.

A term without free variables is said to be *closed*.

The *height* of a term is also defined by structural induction:

- $\text{Height}(x) = 0$,
- $\text{Height}(f(x_1^1 \ \ldots \ x_{k_1}^1 \ t_1, \ \ldots, \ x_1^n \ \ldots \ x_{k_n}^n \ t_n)) = 1 + \max(\text{Height}(t_1), \ \ldots, \ \text{Height} \ (t_n))$.

1.2.5 Substitution

The first operation that we need to define is substitution: indeed, the rôle of variables is not only to be bound but also to be substituted. For example, when we apply the function fun x -> sin (cos (sin x)) to the term 2 * π, at some point we will need to substitute in the term sin (cos (sin x)) the variable x by the term 2 * π.

A *substitution* is simply a mapping from variables to terms, with a finite domain. In other words, a substitution is a finite set of pairs where the first element is a variable and the second a term, and such that each variable occurs at most once as first element in a pair. We can also define a substitution as an association list—$\theta = t_1/x_1 \ \ldots \ t_n/x_n$.

When a substitution is applied to a term, each occurrence of a variable x_1, $\ldots$, x_n in the term is replaced by t_1, $\ldots$, t_n, respectively.

Of course, this replacement only affects the free variables. For example, if we substitute the variable x by the term 2 in the term x + 3, we should obtain the term 2 + 3. However, if we substitute the variable x by the term 2 in the term fun x -> x which represents the identity function we should obtain the term fun x -> x and not fun x -> 2.

The first attempt to define the application of a substitution to a term is as follows:

- $\langle \theta \rangle x_i = t_i$,
- $\langle \theta \rangle x = x$ if x is not in the domain of θ,

$-\ \langle\theta\rangle \texttt{f}(\texttt{y}_1^1\ \ldots\ \texttt{y}_{k_1}^1\ \texttt{u}_1,\ \ldots,\ \texttt{y}_1^n\ \ldots\ \texttt{y}_{k_n}^n\ \texttt{u}_n)\ =\ \texttt{f}(\texttt{y}_1^1\ \ldots$
$\texttt{y}_{k_1}^1\ \langle\theta_{|V\setminus\{\texttt{y}_1^1,\ \ldots,\ \texttt{y}_{k_1}^1\}}\rangle \texttt{u}_1,\ \ldots,\ \texttt{y}_1^n\ \ldots\ \texttt{y}_{k_n}^n\ \langle\theta_{|V\setminus\{\texttt{y}_1^n,\ \ldots,\ \texttt{y}_{k_n}^n\}}\rangle \texttt{u}_n)$

where we use the notation $\theta_{|V\setminus\{\texttt{y}_1,\ \ldots,\ \texttt{y}_k\}}$ for the restriction of the substitution θ to the set $V\setminus\{\texttt{y}_1,\ \ldots,\ \texttt{y}_k\}$, that is, the substitution where we have omitted all the pairs where the first element is one of the variables $\texttt{y}_1,\ \ldots,\ \texttt{y}_k$.

This definition is problematic, because substitutions could *capture variables*. For example, the term `fun x -> (x + y)` represents the function that adds y to its argument. If we substitute y by 4 in this term, we obtain the term `fun x -> (x + 4)` representing the function that adds 4 to its argument. If we substitute y by z, we get the term `fun x -> (x + z)` representing the term that adds z to its argument. But if we substitute y by x, we obtain the function `fun x -> (x + x)` which doubles its argument, instead of the function that adds x to its argument as expected. We can avoid this problem if we change the name of the bound variable: bound variables are dummies, their name does not matter. In other words, in the term `fun x -> (x + y)`, we can replace the bound variable x by any other variable, except of course y. Similarly, when we substitute in the term u the variables $\texttt{x}_1,\ \ldots,\ \texttt{x}_n$ by the terms $\texttt{t}_1,\ \ldots,\ \texttt{t}_n$, we can change the names of the bound variables in u to make sure that their names do not occur in $\texttt{x}_1,\ \ldots,\ \texttt{x}_n$, or in the variables of $\texttt{t}_1,\ \ldots,\ \texttt{t}_n$, or in the variables of u, to avoid capture.

We start by defining an equivalence relation on terms, by induction on the height of terms. This relation is called *alphabetic equivalence*—or *α-equivalence*—and it corresponds to variable renaming.

$-\ \texttt{x} \sim \texttt{x},$
$-\ \texttt{f}(\texttt{y}_1^1\ \ldots\ \texttt{y}_{k_1}^1\ \texttt{t}_1,\ \ldots,\ \texttt{y}_1^n\ \ldots\ \texttt{y}_{k_n}^n\ \texttt{t}_n) \sim \texttt{f}(\texttt{y'}_1^1\ \ldots\ \texttt{y'}_{k_1}^1\ \texttt{t'}_1,$
$\ldots,\ \texttt{y'}_1^n\ \ldots\ \texttt{y'}_{k_n}^n\ \texttt{t'}_n)$ if for all i, and for any sequence of fresh variables $\texttt{z}_1,\ \ldots,\ \texttt{z}_{k_i}$ (that is, variables that do not occur in $\texttt{t}_i, \texttt{t'}_i$), we have $\langle \texttt{z}_1/\texttt{y}_1^i,\ \ldots,\ \texttt{z}_{k_i}/\texttt{y}_{k_i}^i\rangle \texttt{t}_i \sim \langle \texttt{z}_1/\texttt{y'}_1^i,\ \ldots,\ \texttt{z}_{k_i}/\texttt{y'}_{k_i}^i\rangle \texttt{t'}_i.$

For example, the terms `fun x -> x + z` and `fun y -> y + z` are α-equivalent.

In the rest of the book we will work with terms *modulo α-equivalence*, that is, we will consider implicitly α-equivalence classes of terms.

We can now define the operation of substitution by induction on the height of terms:

$-\ \theta\texttt{x}_i\ =\ \texttt{t}_i,$
$-\ \theta\texttt{x}\ =\ \texttt{x}$ if $\texttt{x}$ is not in the domain of θ,
$-\ \theta\texttt{f}(\texttt{y}_1^1\ \ldots\ \texttt{y}_{k_1}^1\ \texttt{u}_1,\ \ldots,\ \texttt{y}_1^n\ \ldots\ \texttt{y}_{k_n}^n\ \texttt{u}_n)\ =\ \texttt{f}(\texttt{z}_1^1\ \ldots$
$\texttt{z}_{k_1}^1\ \theta\langle \texttt{z}_1^1/\texttt{y}_1^1,\ \ldots,\ \texttt{z}_{k_1}^1/\texttt{y}_{k_1}^1\rangle \texttt{u}_1,\ \ldots,\ \texttt{z}_1^n\ \ldots\ \texttt{z}_{k_n}^n\ \theta\langle \texttt{z}_1^n/\texttt{y}_1^n,\ \ldots,$
$\texttt{z}_{k_n}^n/\texttt{y}_{k_n}^n\rangle \texttt{u}_n)$ where $\texttt{z}_1^1,\ \ldots,\ \texttt{z}_{k_1}^1,\ \ldots,\ \texttt{z}_1^n,\ \ldots,\ \texttt{z}_{k_n}^n$ are variables
that do not occur in $\texttt{f}(\texttt{y}_1^1\ \ldots\ \texttt{y}_{k_1}^1\ \texttt{u}_1,\ \ldots,\ \texttt{y}_1^n\ \ldots\ \texttt{y}_{k_n}^n\ \texttt{u}_n)$ or in θ.

For example, if we substitute the variable y by the term `2 * x` in the term `fun x -> x + y`, we obtain the term `fun z -> z + (2 * x)`. The choice of variable z is arbitrary, we could have chosen v or w, and we would have obtained the same term modulo α-equivalence.

The *composition* of the substitutions $\theta = t_1/x_1 \ldots t_n/x_n$ and $\sigma = u_1/y_1 \ldots u_p/y_p$ is the substitution

$$\theta \circ \sigma = \{\theta(\sigma z)/z \mid z \in \{x_1, \ldots, x_n, y_1, \ldots, y_p\}\}$$

We can prove, by induction on the height of t, that for any term t

$$(\theta \circ \sigma)t = \theta(\sigma t)$$

1.3 Three Ways to Define the Semantics of a Language

The semantics of a programming language is a binary relation over the set of terms in the language. Since we have already defined the notion of a language and introduced tools to define relations, we are ready to describe the three main techniques used for semantic definitions. The semantics of a language is usually given as a function, as an inductive definition, or as the reflexive-transitive closure of an explicitly defined relation. They are called *denotational semantics*, *big-step operational semantics* and *small-step operational semantics*, respectively.

1.3.1 Denotational Semantics

Denotational semantics is useful for deterministic languages. In this case, for each program p, the input-output relation defined by a program is a function, written $[\![p]\!]$. The relation $\hookrightarrow$ is then defined by

$$p, e \hookrightarrow s \quad \text{if and only if} \quad [\![p]\!]\, e = s$$

Of course, this simply moves the problem further down: we now need to define the function $[\![p]\!]$. For this, we will use two tools: explicit definitions of functions, and the fixed point theorem... but we will leave this for later.

1.3.2 Big-Step Operational Semantics

The big-step operational semantics is also called *structural operational semantics* (S.O.S.) or *natural semantics*. It gives an inductive definition of the relation $\hookrightarrow$.

1.3.3 Small-Step Operational Semantics

The small-step operational semantics is also called *reduction semantics*. It defines the relation $\hookrightarrow$ by means of another relation $\triangleright$ that describes the basic steps to transform the initial term t into the final term s.

For example, when we run the program `fun x -> (x * x) + x` with input 4, we obtain the result 20. But the term `(fun x -> (x * x) + x) 4` does not become 20 in one step, it is first transformed into `(4 * 4) + 4`, then `16 + 4`, and finally 20.

The most important relation is not the one that links `(fun x -> (x * x) + x) 4` with 20, but ▷, which relates the term `(fun x -> (x * x) + x) 4` with `(4 * 4) + 4`, then the term `(4 * 4) + 4` with `16 + 4` and finally the term `16 + 4` with the term 20.

Once the relation ▷ is given, ↪ can be derived from the reflexive-transitive closure ▷* of the relation ▷

$$t \hookrightarrow s \quad \text{if and only if} \quad t \vartriangleright^* s \text{ and } s \text{ is irreducible}$$

The fact that the term s is irreducible implies that there is nothing else to compute in s. For example, the term 20 is irreducible, but the term `16 + 4` is not. A term *s* is irreducible if there is no term s' such that s ▷ s'.

1.3.4 Non-termination

The execution of a program may produce a result, produce an error, or never terminate. Errors can be seen as particular kinds of results. For non-terminating programs, there are several ways to define a semantics. A first alternative is to consider that if the term t does not terminate, then there is no pair (t, s) in the relation ↪. Another alternative is to add a specific element ⊥ to the set of output values, and to state that the relation ↪ contains the pair (t, ⊥) when the term t does not terminate.

The difference may seem superficial: it is easy to delete all the pairs of the form (t, ⊥), or to add such a pair if there is no pair of the form (t, s) in the relation. However, readers who are familiar with computability problems will notice that, if we add the pairs (t, ⊥), the relation ↪ is no longer recursively enumerable.

Chapter 2
The Language PCF

We will illustrate the various styles of semantics of programming languages with an example: the language PCF—*Programming language for computable functions*—, also called Mini-ML.

2.1 A Functional Language: PCF

2.1.1 Programs Are Functions

We observed in the previous chapter that a deterministic program computes a function, and from this observation we derived the principles of denotational semantics. This remark is also the basis of a class of programming languages: functional languages, such as Caml, Haskell or Lisp, which are traditionally used to begin the study of programming languages.

In these languages, the goal is to shorten the distance between the notion of a program and the notion of a mathematical function. In other words, the idea is to bring programs closer to their denotational semantics.

The basic constructions in the language PCF are the *explicit construction* of a function, written `fun x -> t`, and the *application* of a function to an argument, written `t u`.

PCF includes also a constant for each natural number, the operations `+`, `-`, `*`, `/`, and a test to detect zero `ifz t then u else v`. Addition and multiplication are defined for all natural numbers, and similarly for subtraction using the convention $n - m = 0$ if $n < m$. Division is the standard Euclidean division, division by 0 produces an error.

2.1.2 Functions Are First-Class Objects

In many programming languages, it is possible to define a function that takes another function as argument, or that returns another function, but often this requires the use

G. Dowek, J.-J. Lévy, *Introduction to the Theory of Programming Languages*,
Undergraduate Topics in Computer Science,
DOI 10.1007/978-0-85729-076-2_2, © Springer-Verlag London Limited 2011

of a syntax that is different from the syntax used for a standard argument such as an integer or a string. In a functional language, functions are defined in the same way whether they take numbers or functions as arguments.

For example, the composition of a function with itself is defined by `fun f -> fun x -> f (f x)`.

To highlight the fact that functions are not considered different, and thus they can be used as arguments or returned as results for other functions, we say that functions are *first class objects*.

2.1.3 Functions with Several Arguments

In PCF, there is no symbol to build a function with several arguments. These functions are built as functions with one argument, using the isomorphism `(A × B) -> C = A -> (B -> C)`. For instance, the function that associates to x and y the number `x * x + y * y` is defined as the function associating to x a function, which in turn associates to y the number `x * x + y * y`, that is, `fun x -> fun y -> x * x + y * y`.

Then, to apply the function `f` to the numbers 3 and 4 we need to apply it first to 3, obtaining the term `f 3`, which represents the function that associates `3 * 3 + y * y` to y, and then to 4, obtaining the term `(f 3) 4`. Since, by convention, application associates to the left, we will write this term simply as `f 3 4`.

2.1.4 No Assignments

In contrast with languages such as Caml or Java, the main feature of PCF is a total lack of *assignments*. There is no construction of the form `x := t` or `x = t` to assign a value to a "variable". We will describe, in Chap. 7, an extension of PCF with assignments.

2.1.5 Recursive Definitions

In Mathematics, some functions cannot be defined explicitly. For example, in a high-school textbook, the power function is often defined by

$$x, \ n \mapsto \underbrace{x \, x \cdots x \, x}_{n \text{ times}}$$

or through a definition by induction.

In programming languages, we use similar constructs: iterations and recursive definitions. PCF includes a special construct to define recursive functions.

It is often said that a function is recursive if the function is used in its own definition. This is absurd: in programming languages, as everywhere else, circular definitions are meaningless. We cannot "define" the function `fact` by `fun n -> ifz n then 1 else n * (fact (n - 1))`. In general, we cannot define a function `f` by a term `G` which contains an occurrence of `f`. However, we can define the function `f` as the fixed point of the function `fun f -> G`. For example, we can define the function `fact` as the fixed point of the function `fun f -> fun n -> ifz n then 1 else n * (f (n - 1))`.

Does this function have a fixed point? and if it does, is this fixed point unique? Otherwise, which fixed point are we referring to? We will leave these questions for a moment, and simply state that a recursive function is defined as a fixed point.

In PCF, the symbol `fix` binds a variable in its argument, and the term `fix f G` denotes the fixed point of the function `fun f -> G`. The function `fact` can then be defined by `fix f fun n -> ifz n then 1 else n * (f (n - 1))`.

Note, again, that using the symbol `fix` we can build the factorial function without necessarily giving it a name.

2.1.6 Definitions

We could, in theory, omit definitions and replace everywhere the defined symbols by their definitions. However, programs are simpler and clearer if we use definitions.

We add then a final construct in PCF, written `let x = t in u`. The occurrences of the variable `x` in `u` are bound, but those in `t` are not. The symbol `let` is a binary operator that binds a variable in its second argument.

2.1.7 The Language PCF

The language PCF contains

- a symbol `fun` with one argument, that binds a variable in its argument,
- a symbol α with two arguments, which does not bind any variables in its arguments,
- an infinite number of constants to represent the natural numbers,
- four symbols +, -, * and / with two arguments, which do not bind any variables in their arguments,
- a symbol `ifz` with three arguments, which does not bind any variables in its arguments,
- a symbol `fix` with one argument, which binds a variable in its argument,
- a symbol `let` with two arguments, which binds a variable in its second argument.

In other words, the syntax of PCF is inductively defined by

```
t = x
  | fun x -> t
  | t t
  | n
  | t + t | t - t | t * t | t / t
  | ifz t then t else t
  | fix x t
  | let x = t in t
```

Despite its small size, PCF is Turing complete, that is, all computable functions can be programmed in PCF.

Exercise 2.1 Write a PCF program that takes two natural numbers n and p as inputs and returns n^p.

Exercise 2.2 Write a PCF program that takes a natural number n as input and returns the number 1 if the input is a prime number, and 0 otherwise.

Exercise 2.3 (Polynomials in PCF) Write a PCF program that takes a natural number q as input, and returns the greatest natural number u such that u $(u + 1)$ $/$ $2 \leq q$.

Cantor's function K is a function from $\mathbb{N}^2$ to $\mathbb{N}$ defined by fun n -> fun p -> $(n + p)$ $(n + p + 1)$ $/$ $2 + n$. Let K' be the function from $\mathbb{N}$ to $\mathbb{N}^2$ defined by fun q -> $(q - (u (u + 1) / 2), u - q + u (u + 1) / 2)$ where u is the greatest natural number such that u $(u + 1)$ $/$ $2 \leq q$.

Show that $K \circ K' = \mathrm{id}$. Let n and p be two natural numbers, show that the greatest natural number u such that u $(u + 1)$ $/$ $2 \leq (n + p)$ $(n + p + 1)$ $/$ $2 + n$ is $n + p$. Then deduce that $K' \circ K = \mathrm{id}$. From this fact, deduce that K is a bijection from $\mathbb{N}^2$ to $\mathbb{N}$.

Let L be the function fun n -> fun p -> $(K\ n\ p)$ $+ 1$. A polynomial with integer coefficients $a_0 + a_1 X + \cdots + a_i X^i + \cdots + a_n X^n$ can be represented by the integer L a_0 (L a_1 (L a_2 ... (L a_n 0) ...)).

Write a PCF program that takes two natural numbers as input and returns the value of the polynomial represented by the first number applied to the second.

2.2 Small-Step Operational Semantics for PCF

2.2.1 Rules

Let us apply the program fun x -> 2 * x to the constant 3. We obtain the term (fun x -> 2 * x) 3. According to the principles of small-step operational semantics, let us try to evaluate this term step by step, to obtain a result: 6 if all goes well. The first step in this simplification process is *parameter passing*, that is, the replacement of the formal argument x by the actual argument 3. The initial term becomes, after a first small-step transformation, the term 2 * 3. In the second step, the term 2 * 3 is evaluated, resulting in the number 6. The first small step, parameter passing, can be performed each time we have a term of the form (fun x -> t) u where a function fun x -> t is applied to an argument u. As a consequence, we define the following rule, called *β-reduction rule*

$$(\text{fun } x \rightarrow t) \ u \longrightarrow (u/x)t$$

The relation t $\longrightarrow$ u should be read "t reduces—or rewrites—to u". The second step mentioned above can be generalised as follows

$$p \otimes q \longrightarrow n \text{ (if } p \otimes q = n)$$

where $\otimes$ is any of the four arithmetic operators included in PCF. We add similar rules for conditionals

$$\text{ifz } 0 \text{ then } t \text{ else } u \longrightarrow t$$

$$\text{ifz } n \text{ then } t \text{ else } u \longrightarrow u \text{ (if } n \text{ is a number different from 0)}$$

a rule for fixed points

$$\text{fix } x \ t \longrightarrow (\text{fix } x \ t/x)t$$

and a rule for let

$$\text{let } x = t \text{ in } u \longrightarrow (t/x)u$$

A *redex* is a term t that can be reduced. In other words, a term t is a redex if there exists a term u such that t $\longrightarrow$ u.

2.2.2 Numbers

It could be said, quite rightly, that the rule $p \otimes q \longrightarrow n$ (if $p \otimes q = n$), of which 2 * 3 $\longrightarrow$ 6 is an instance, does not really explain the semantics of the arithmetic operators, since it just replaces the multiplication in PCF by that of Mathematics. This choice is however motivated by the fact that we are not really interested in the semantics of arithmetic operators, instead, our goal is to highlight the semantics of the other constructs in the language.

To define the semantics of the arithmetic operators in PCF without referring to the mathematical operators, we should consider a variant of PCF without numeric constants, where we introduce just one constant for the number 0 and a symbol S—"successor"—with one argument. The number 3, for instance, is represented by the term S(S(S(0))). We then add small-step rules

$$0 + u \longrightarrow u$$
$$S(t) + u \longrightarrow S(t + u)$$
$$0 - u \longrightarrow 0$$

```
t - 0 ⟶ t
S(t) - S(u) ⟶ t - u
0 * u ⟶ 0
S(t) * u ⟶ t * u + u
t / S(u) ⟶ ifz t - u then 0 else S((t - S(u)) / S(u))
```

Note that, to be precise, we should add a rule for division by 0, which should raise an exception: error.

Exercise 2.4 (Church numerals) Instead of introducing the symbols 0 and S, we can represent the number n by the term fun z -> fun s -> s (s (... (s z)...)) rather than S(S(...(0)...)). Show that addition and multiplication can be programmed on these representations. Show that the function that checks whether a number is 0 can also be programmed.

Exercise 2.5 (Position numerals) It could be said that the representations of numbers using the symbols 0 and S, or using Church numerals, are not efficient, since the size of the term representing a number grows linearly with the number—as the representation in unary notation, where to write the number n we need n symbols—and not logarithmically, as it is the case with the usual position-based notation. An alternative could be to use a symbol z for the number 0 and two functions O and I to represent the functions $n \mapsto 2 * n$ and $n \mapsto 2 * n + 1$. The number 26 would then be represented by the term O(I(O(I(I(z))))), and reversing it we obtain IIOIO, the binary representation of this number.

Write a small-step operational semantics for the arithmetic operators in this language.

2.2.3 A Congruence

Using the rules of the small-step semantics we obtain

$$(fun \ x \ -> \ 2 \ * \ x) \ 3 \ \longrightarrow \ 2 \ * \ 3 \ \longrightarrow \ 6$$

Thus, denoting by $\longrightarrow^*$ the reflexive-transitive closure of $\longrightarrow$, we can write (fun x -> 2 * x) 3 $\longrightarrow^*$ 6.

However, with this definition, the term (2 + 3) + 4 does not reduce to the term 9 according to $\longrightarrow^*$. Indeed, to reduce a term of the form t + u the terms t and u should be numeric constants, but our first term 2 + 3 is a sum, not a constant. The first step should then be the evaluation of 2 + 3, which produces the number 5. Then, a second step reduces 5 + 4 to 9. The problem is that, with our definition, the term 2 + 3 reduces to 5, but (2 + 3) + 4 does not reduce to 5 + 4.

We need to define another relation, where rules can be applied to any subterm of a term to be reduced. Let us define inductively the relation ▷ as follows

$$\frac{}{t \ ▷ \ u} \quad \text{if } t \ \longrightarrow \ u$$

$$\frac{t \rhd u}{t\ v \rhd u\ v}$$

$$\frac{t \rhd u}{v\ t \rhd v\ u}$$

$$\frac{t \rhd u}{\text{fun}\ x \to t \rhd \text{fun}\ x \to u}$$

$$\frac{t \rhd u}{t\ +\ v \rhd u\ +\ v}$$

$$\ldots$$

It is possible to show that a term is a redex with respect to the relation $\rhd$ if and only if one of its subterms is a redex with respect to $\longrightarrow$.

2.2.4 An Example

To illustrate PCF's small-step semantic rules, let us compute the factorial of 3.

```
(fix f fun n -> ifz n then 1 else n * (f (n - 1))) 3
 ⊳ (fun n -> ifz n then 1 else n * ((fix f fun n ->
ifz n then 1 else n * (f (n - 1))) (n - 1))) 3
 ⊳ ifz 3 then 1 else 3 * ((fix f fun n -> ifz n then 1
else n * (f (n - 1))) (3 - 1))
 ⊳ 3 * ((fix f fun n -> ifz n then 1 else
n * (f (n - 1))) (3 - 1))
 ⊳ 3 * ((fix f fun n -> ifz n then 1 else
n * (f (n - 1))) 2)
 ⊳ 3 * ((fun n -> ifz n then 1 else n * ((fix f fun n ->
ifz n then 1 else n * (f (n - 1))) (n - 1))) 2)
 ⊳ 3 * (ifz 2 then 1 else 2 * ((fix f fun n -> ifz n
then 1 else n * (f (n - 1))) (2 - 1)))
 ⊳ 3 * (2 * ((fix f fun n -> ifz n then 1 else
n * (f (n - 1))) (2 - 1)))
 ⊳ 3 * (2 * ((fix f fun n -> ifz n then 1 else
n * (f (n - 1))) 1))
 ⊳ 3 * (2 * ((fun n -> ifz n then 1 else
n * ((fix f fun n -> ifz n then 1 else
n * (f (n - 1))) (n - 1))) 1))
 ⊳ 3 * (2 * (ifz 1 then 1 else 1 * ((fix f fun n ->
ifz n then 1 else n * (f (n - 1))) (1 - 1))))
 ⊳ 3 * (2 * (1 * ((fix f fun n -> ifz n then 1 else
n * (f (n - 1))) (1 - 1))))
```

```
▷ 3 * (2 * (1 * ((fix f fun n -> ifz n then 1
else n * (f (n - 1))) 0)))
▷ 3 * (2 * (1 * ((fun n -> ifz n then 1 else
n * ((fix f fun n -> ifz n then 1 else
n * (f (n - 1))) (n - 1))) 0)))
▷ 3 * (2 * (1 * ((ifz 0 then 1 else
0 * ((fix f fun n -> ifz n then 1 else
n * (f (n - 1))) (0 - 1))))))
▷ 3 * (2 * (1 * 1)) ▷ 3 * (2 * 1) ▷ 3 * 2 ▷ 6
```

2.2.5 Irreducible Closed Terms

A term t is *irreducible* if it cannot be reduced by ▷, that is, if there is no term u such that t ▷ u.

We can now define the relation "the term u is the result of the evaluation of term t", where t is a closed term, by: t ↪ u if and only if t ▷* u and u is irreducible. In this case, the term u must be closed. Finally, the relation "the program p with inputs $e_1, \ldots, e_n$ produces the output s" is simply written p $e_1 \ldots e_n$ ↪ s.

Exercise 2.6 (Classification of irreducible closed terms) Show that a term is irreducible and closed if and only if it is of one of the following forms

- fun x -> t where t is irreducible and does not contain any free variables except possibly x,
- n where n is a number,
- $V_1 V_2$, where V_1 and V_2 are irreducible closed terms and V_1 is not of the form fun x -> t,
- $V_1 \otimes V_2$, where V_1 and V_2 are irreducible closed terms and are not both numeric constants,
- ifz V_1 then V_2 else V_3 where V_1, V_2 and V_3 are irreducible closed terms and V_1 is not a number.

Numbers and irreducible closed terms of the form fun x -> t are called *values*. When the result of a computation is a value, we associate the value to the initial term, and we say that the term *evaluates* to this value.

Unfortunately, values are not the only possible results. For example, the term (fun x -> x) 1 2 can be reduced to the term 1 2, which is irreducible and closed, and thus the term 1 2 is the result of the computation of (fun x -> x) 1 2. This result is meaningless, because we cannot apply the object 1, which is not a function, to 2. An irreducible closed term that is not a value is said to be *stuck*. Stuck terms have the form $V_1 V_2$, where V_1 and V_2 are irreducible closed terms and V_1 is not a function fun x -> t (for example 1 2), $V_1 \otimes V_2$, where V_1 and V_2 are irreducible and closed and are not numbers (for example 1 +

(fun ' x -> x)), and ifz V₁ then V₂ else V₃ where V_1, V_2 and V_3 are irreducible and closed and V_1 is not a number (for example, ifz (fun x -> x) then 1 else 2).

Exercise 2.7 Which are the values associated to the terms

(fun x -> fun x -> x) 2 3

and

(fun x -> fun y -> ((fun x -> (x + y)) x)) 5 4

according to the small-step operational semantics of PCF?

Exercise 2.8 (Static binding) Does the small-step operational semantics of PCF associate the value 10 or the value 11 to the term

let x = 4 in let f = fun y -> y + x
in let x = 5 in f 6?

The first versions of the language Lisp produced the value 11 instead of 10 for this term. In this case, we say that the binding is *dynamic*.

2.2.6 Non-termination

It is easy to see that the relation $\hookrightarrow$ is not total, that is, there are terms t for which there is no term u such that t $\hookrightarrow$ u. For example, the term b = fix x x reduces to itself, and only to itself. It does not reduce to any irreducible term.

Exercise 2.9 Let b_1 = (fix f (fun x -> (f x))) 0. Show all the terms obtained by reducing this term. Does the computation produce a result in this case?

Exercise 2.10 (Curry's fixed point operator) Let t be a term and u be the term (fun y -> (t (y y))) (fun y -> (t (y y))). Show that u reduces to t u.

Let t be a term and v be the term (fun y -> ((fun x -> t) (y y))) (fun y -> ((fun x -> t) (y y))). Show that v reduces to (v/x) t.

Thus, we can deduce that the symbol fix is superfluous in PCF. However, it is not going to be superfluous later when we add types to PCF.

Write a term u without using the symbol fix and equivalent to b = fix x x. Describe the terms that can be obtained by reduction. Does the computation produce a result in this case?

2.2.7 Confluence

Is it possible for a closed term to produce several results? And, in general, can a term reduce to several different irreducible terms? The answer to these questions is negative. In fact, every PCF program is deterministic, but this is not a trivial property. Let us see why.

The term $(3 + 4) + (5 + 6)$ has two subterms which are both redexes. We could then start by reducing $3 + 4$ to 7 or $5 + 6$ to 11. Indeed, the term $(3 + 4) + (5 + 6)$ reduces to both $7 + (5 + 6)$ and $(3 + 4) + 11$. Fortunately, neither of these terms is irreducible, and if we continue the computation we reach in both cases the term 18.

To prove that any term can be reduced to at most one irreducible term we need to prove that if two computations originating in the same term produce different terms, then they will eventually reach the same irreducible term.

This property is a consequence of another property of the relation $\triangleright$: *confluence*. A relation R is confluent if each time we have a R^* b_1 and a R^* b_2, there exists some c such that b_1 R^* c and b_2 R^* c.

It is not difficult to show that confluence implies that each term has at most one irreducible result. If the term t can be reduced to two irreducible terms u_1 and u_2, then we have t $\triangleright^*$ u_1 and t $\triangleright^*$ u_2. Since $\triangleright$ is confluent, there exists a term v such that $u_1 \triangleright^*$ v and $u_2 \triangleright^*$ v. Since u_1 is irreducible, the only term v such that $u_1 \triangleright^*$ v is u_1 itself. Therefore, $u_1 = $ v and similarly $u_2 = $ v. We conclude that $u_1 = u_2$. In other words, t reduces to at most one irreducible term.

We will not give here the proof of confluence for the relation $\triangleright$. The idea is that when a term t contains two redexes r_1 and r_2, and t_1 is obtained by reducing r_1 and t_2 is obtained by reducing r_2, then we can find the residuals of r_2 in t_1 and reduce them. Similarly, we can reduce the residuals of r_1 in t_2, obtaining the same term. For example, by reducing $5 + 6$ in $7 + (5 + 6)$ and reducing $3 + 4$ in $(3 + 4) + 11$, we obtain the same term: $7 + 11$.

2.3   Reduction Strategies

2.3.1 The Notion of a Strategy

Since in PCF each term has at most one result (due to the unicity property mentioned above), it does not matter in which order we reduce the redexes in a term: if we reach an irreducible term, it will always be the same. However, it may be the case that one sequence of reduction reaches an irreducible term whereas another one does not. For example, let C be the term `fun x -> 0` and let b_1 be the term `(fix f (fun x -> (f x))) 0`. The term b_1 reduces to $b_2 = $ `(fun x -> (fix f (fun x -> (f x)) x)) 0` and then again to b_1. The term C b_1 contains several redexes, and it can be reduced to 0 and to C b_2 which in turn contains several redexes and can be reduced to 0 and C b_1 (amongst other terms). By reducing always the innermost redex, we can build an infinite reduction sequence C b_1 ▷ C b_2 ▷ C b_1 ▷ $\cdots$, whereas reducing the outermost redex produces the result 0.

This example may seem an exception, because it contains a function C that does not use its argument; but note that the ifz construct is similar, and in the example of the factorial function, when computing the factorial of 3 for instance, we can observe the same behaviour: The term ifz 0 then 1 else 0 * ((fix f fun n -> ifz n then 1 else n * (f (n - 1))) (0 - 1)) has several redexes. Outermost reduction produces the result 1 (the other redexes disappear), whereas reducing the redex fix f fun n -> ifz n then 1 else n * (f (n - 1)) we get an infinite reduction sequence. In other words, the term fact 3 can be reduced to 6, but it can also generate reductions that go on forever.

Both C b_1 and fact 3 produce a unique result, but not all reduction sequences reach a result.

Since the term C b_1 has the value 0 according to the PCF semantics, an *evaluator*, that is, a program that takes as input a PCF term and returns its value, should produce the result 0 when computing C b_1. Let us try to evaluate this term using some current compilers. In Caml, the program

```
let rec f x = f x in let g x = 0 in g (f 0)
```

does not terminate. In Java, we have the same problem with the program

```
class Omega {
  static int f (int x) {return f(x);}
  static int g (int x) {return 0;}
  static public void main (String [ ] args) {
  System.out.println(g(f(0)));}}
```

Only a small number of compilers, using *call by name* or *lazy* evaluation, such as Haskell, Lazy-ML or Gaml, produce a terminating program for this term.

This is because the small-step semantics of PCF does not correspond to the semantics of Caml or Java. In fact, it is too general and when a term has several redexes it does not specify which one should be reduced first. By default, it imposes termination of all programs that somehow can produce a result. An ingredient is missing in this semantic definition: the notion of a strategy, that specifies the order of reduction of redexes.

A *strategy* is a partial function that associates to each term in its domain one of its redex occurrences. Given a strategy s, we can define another semantics, replacing the relation ▷ by a new relation ▷$_s$ such that t ▷$_s$ u if s t is defined and u is obtained by reducing the redex s t in t. Then, we define the relation ▷$_s^*$ as the reflexive-transitive closure of ▷$_s$, and the relation $\hookrightarrow_s$ as before.

Instead of defining a strategy, an alternative would be to weaken the reduction rules, in particular the congruence rules, so that only some specific reductions can be performed.

2.3.2 Weak Reduction

Before defining outermost or innermost strategies for the term C b_1, let us give another example to show that the operational semantics defined above is too liberal, and to motivate the definition of strategies or weaker reduction rules. Let us apply the program `fun x -> x + (4 + 5)` to the constant 3. We obtain the term `(fun x -> x + (4 + 5)) 3` that contains two redexes. We can then reduce it to `3 + (4 + 5)` or to `(fun x -> x + 9) 3`. The first reduction is part of the execution of the program, but not the second. Usually, if we execute a function before passing arguments to it, we say that we are *optimising* or *specialising* the program.

A *weak reduction strategy* never reduces a redex that is under a `fun`. Thus, weak reduction does not specialise programs, it just executes them. It follows that with a weak strategy all terms of the form `fun x -> t` are irreducible.

Alternatively, we can define weak reduction by weakening the reduction rules, more precisely, by discarding the congruence rule

$$\frac{t \ \triangleright \ u}{\texttt{fun x -> t} \ \triangleright \ \texttt{fun x -> u}}$$

Exercise 2.11 (Classification of weak irreducible closed terms) Show that, under weak reduction, a closed irreducible term must have one of the following forms:

– `fun x -> t`, where t has at most x free,
– n where n is a number,
– $V_1 \ V_2$, where V_1 and V_2 are irreducible closed terms and V_1 is not a term of the form `fun x -> t`,
– $V_1 \otimes V_2$, where V_1 and V_2 are irreducible closed terms and are not both numbers,
– `ifz` V_1 `then` V_2 `else` V_3 where V_1, V_2 and V_3 are irreducible closed terms and V_1 is not a number.

What is the difference with Exercise 2.6?

Numbers and closed terms of the form `fun x -> t` are called *values*.

2.3.3 Call by Name

Let us analyse again the reductions available for the term C b_1. We need to decide whether we should evaluate the arguments of the function C before they are passed to the function, or we should pass to the function the arguments without evaluating them.

The *call by name* strategy always reduces the leftmost redex first, and the weak call by name strategy always reduces the leftmost redex that is not under a `fun`. Thus, the term C b_1 reduces to 0. This strategy is interesting due to the following property, called standardisation: if a term can be reduced to an irreducible term, then the call by name strategy terminates. In other words, $\hookrightarrow_n$ = $\hookrightarrow$. Moreover, when we evaluate the term (fun x -> 0) (fact 10) using a call by name strategy, we do not need to compute the factorial of 10. However, if we evaluate the term (fun x -> x + x) (fact 10), using a call by name strategy, we will compute it twice, because this term reduces to (fact 10) + (fact 10). Most call by name evaluators use sharing to avoid this duplication of computation, and in this case we call it *lazy* evaluation.

2.3.4 Call by Value

Call by value, in contrast, always evaluates the arguments of a function before passing them to the function. It is based on the following convention: we can only reduce a term of the form (fun x -> t) u if u is a value. Thus, when we evaluate the term (fun x -> x + x) (fact 10), we start by reducing the argument to obtain (fun x -> x + x) 3628800, and then we reduce the leftmost redex. By doing this, we only compute the factorial of 10 once.

All the strategies that evaluate arguments before passing them are in this class. For instance, the strategy that reduces always the leftmost redex amongst those that are authorised. Thus, call by value is not a unique strategy, but a family of strategies.

This convention can also be defined by weakening the β-reduction rule: the term (fun x -> t) u is a redex only if the term u is a value.

A weak strategy is said to implement call by value if it reduces a term of the form (fun x -> t) u only when u is a value and is not under a fun.

2.3.5 A Bit of Laziness Is Needed

Even under a call by value strategy, a conditional construct ifz must be evaluated under call by name: in a term of the form ifz t then u else v, we should never evaluate the three arguments. Instead, we should first evaluate t and depending on the result, evaluate either u or v.

It is easy to see that if we evaluate the three arguments of an ifz then the evaluation of the term fact 3 does not terminate.

Exercise 2.12 Characterise the irreducible closed terms under weak call by name, then characterise the irreducible closed terms under weak call by value.

2.4 Big-Step Operational Semantics for PCF

Instead of defining a strategy, or weakening the reduction rules of the small-step operational semantics, we can control the order in which redexes are reduced by defining a *big-step* operational semantics.

The big-step operational semantics of a programming language provides an inductive definition of the relation $\hookrightarrow$, without first defining $\longrightarrow$ and $\triangleright$.

2.4.1 Call by Name

Let us start by the call by name semantics for PCF. Consider a term of the form t u that is reduced under call by name to obtain an irreducible term V. We will start by reducing the redexes that occur in t until we obtain an irreducible term. If this term is of the form `fun x -> t'`, then the whole term reduces to `(fun x -> t')` u and the left-most redex is the term itself. It reduces to `(u/x)t'`, which in turn reduces to V. We can say that the term t u reduces under call by name to the irreducible term V if t reduces to `fun x -> t'` and `(u/x)t'` reduces to V.

This can be expressed as a rule

$$\frac{\text{t} \hookrightarrow \text{fun x -> t'} \qquad \text{(u/x)t'} \hookrightarrow \text{V}}{\text{t u} \hookrightarrow \text{V}}$$

which will be part of the inductive definition of the relation $\hookrightarrow$ (without first defining $\longrightarrow$ and $\triangleright$).

Other rules state that the result of the computation for a term of the form `fun` is the term itself, that is, we are defining a weak reduction relation

$$\overline{\text{fun x -> t} \hookrightarrow \text{fun x -> t}}$$

and that the result of the computation of a term of the form n is the term itself

$$\overline{\text{n} \hookrightarrow \text{n}}$$

Also, there is a rule to give the semantics of arithmetic operators

$$\frac{\text{u} \hookrightarrow \text{q} \qquad \text{t} \hookrightarrow \text{p}}{\text{t} \otimes \text{u} \hookrightarrow \text{n}} \text{ if } \text{p} \otimes \text{q} = \text{n}$$

two rules to define the semantics of the `ifz` construct

$$\frac{\text{t} \hookrightarrow \text{0} \qquad \text{u} \hookrightarrow \text{V}}{\text{ifz t then u else v} \hookrightarrow \text{V}}$$

$$\frac{\text{t} \hookrightarrow \text{n} \qquad \text{v} \hookrightarrow \text{V}}{\text{ifz t then u else v} \hookrightarrow \text{V}} \begin{array}{l} \text{if n is a} \\ \text{number} \neq 0 \end{array}$$

a rule to define the semantics of the fixed point operator

$$\frac{\text{(fix x t/x)t} \hookrightarrow \text{V}}{\text{fix x t} \hookrightarrow \text{V}}$$

and finally a rule to define the semantics of a `let`

$$\frac{\texttt{(t/x)u} \hookrightarrow \texttt{V}}{\texttt{let x = t in u} \hookrightarrow \texttt{V}}$$

We can prove by structural induction on the evaluation relation that the result of the computation of a term is always a value, that is, a number or a closed term of the form `fun`. There are no stuck terms. The computation of a term such as `((fun x -> x) 1) 2`, which gave rise to the term `1 2` (stuck) with the small-step semantics, does not produce a result with the big-step semantics, since none of the rules can be applied to this term. Indeed, there is no rule in the big-step semantics that explains how to evaluate an application where the left part evaluates to a number.

2.4.2 Call by Value

The rules defining the call by value semantics are similar, except for the application rule: we compute the value of the argument before passing it to the function

$$\frac{\texttt{u} \hookrightarrow \texttt{W} \qquad \texttt{t} \hookrightarrow \texttt{fun x -> t'} \qquad \texttt{(W/x)t'} \hookrightarrow \texttt{V}}{\texttt{t u} \hookrightarrow \texttt{V}}$$

and the `let` rule

$$\frac{\texttt{t} \hookrightarrow \texttt{W} \qquad \texttt{(W/x)u} \hookrightarrow \texttt{V}}{\texttt{let x = t in u} \hookrightarrow \texttt{V}}$$

Summarising, we have the following rules

$$\frac{\texttt{u} \hookrightarrow \texttt{W} \qquad \texttt{t} \hookrightarrow \texttt{fun x -> t'} \qquad \texttt{(W/x)t'} \hookrightarrow \texttt{V}}{\texttt{t u} \hookrightarrow \texttt{V}}$$

$$\frac{}{\texttt{fun x -> t} \hookrightarrow \texttt{fun x -> t}}$$

$$\frac{}{\texttt{n} \hookrightarrow \texttt{n}}$$

$$\frac{\texttt{u} \hookrightarrow \texttt{q} \qquad \texttt{t} \hookrightarrow \texttt{p}}{\texttt{t} \otimes \texttt{u} \hookrightarrow \texttt{n}} \text{ if } p \otimes q = n$$

$$\frac{\texttt{t} \hookrightarrow \texttt{0} \qquad \texttt{u} \hookrightarrow \texttt{V}}{\texttt{ifz t then u else v} \hookrightarrow \texttt{V}}$$

$$\frac{\texttt{t} \hookrightarrow \texttt{n} \qquad \texttt{v} \hookrightarrow \texttt{V}}{\texttt{ifz t then u else v} \hookrightarrow \texttt{V}} \begin{array}{l} \text{if } n \text{ is a} \\ \text{constant} \neq 0 \end{array}$$

$$\frac{(\text{fix x t/x})t \hookrightarrow V}{\text{fix x t} \hookrightarrow V}$$

$$\frac{t \hookrightarrow W \qquad (W/x)u \hookrightarrow V}{\text{let x} = t \text{ in u} \hookrightarrow V}$$

Notice that, even under call by value, we keep the rules for the ifz

$$\frac{t \hookrightarrow 0 \qquad u \hookrightarrow V}{\text{ifz t then u else v} \hookrightarrow V}$$

$$\frac{t \hookrightarrow n \qquad v \hookrightarrow V}{\text{ifz t then u else v} \hookrightarrow V} \quad \begin{array}{l} \text{if n is a} \\ \text{constant} \neq 0 \end{array}$$

that is, we do not evaluate the second and third arguments of an ifz until they are needed.

Note also that, even under call by value, we keep the rule

$$\frac{(\text{fix x t/x})t \hookrightarrow V}{\text{fix x t} \hookrightarrow V}$$

We must resist the temptation to evaluate the term fix x t to a value W before substituting it in t, because the rule

$$\frac{\text{fix x t} \hookrightarrow W \qquad (W/x)t \hookrightarrow V}{\text{fix x t} \hookrightarrow V}$$

requires, in order to evaluate fix x t, to start by evaluating fix x t which would create a loop and the term fact 3 would never produce a value—its evaluation would give rise to an infinite computation.

Note finally that other rule combinations are possible. For example, some variants of the call by name semantics use call by value in the let rule.

Exercise 2.13 Which values do we obtain under big-step semantics for the terms

```
(fun x -> fun x -> x) 2 3
```

and

```
(fun x -> fun y -> ((fun x -> (x + y)) x)) 5 4?
```

Compare your answer with that of Exercise 2.7.

Exercise 2.14 Does the big-step semantics associate the value 10 or the value 11 to the term

```
let x = 4 in let f = fun y -> y + x
in let x = 5 in f 6?
```

Compare your answer with that of Exercise 2.8.

2.5 Evaluation of PCF Programs

A PCF evaluator is a program that takes a closed PCF term as input, and produces its value as output. When read in a bottom-up fashion, the rules in the big-step semantics can be seen as the kernel of such an evaluator: To evaluate an application t u one starts by evaluating u and t, ... this is easy to program in a language like Caml

```
let rec eval p = match p with
| App(t,u) -> let w = eval u
              in let v = eval t
              in ...
| ...
```

In the case of an application, the rules of the big-step semantics leave us the freedom to evaluate u first or t first—call by value is not a strategy, but a family of strategies—, but the term $(W/x) t'$ must be the third to be evaluated, because it is built out of the results of the first two evaluations.

Exercise 2.15 Write a call by name evaluator for PCF, that is, a program that takes as input a closed term and computes its value. Write a call by value evaluator. Evaluate the term fact 6 and the term C b_1 in both cases.

PCF's denotational semantics is more difficult to define. This may seem a paradox, since PCF is a functional language and it should be easy to interpret its programs as functions. However, in PCF, any object can be applied to any object, and nothing stops us writing for instance the term fun x -> (x x). In contrast with mathematical functions, PCF functions do not have a domain. For this reasons, we will give a denotational semantics for PCF after we add types, in Chap. 5.

Chapter 3
From Evaluation to Interpretation

3.1 Call by Name

Using the rules of the big-step operational semantics, we can build an evaluator for PCF where a term of the form (fun x -> t) u is evaluated by first substituting the variable x by the term u everywhere in the body t of the function. For example, to evaluate the term (fun x -> (x * x) + x) 4, we substitute x by 4 in the term (x * x) + x and then we evaluate the term (4 * 4) + 4. Substitutions are costly operations; to increase the efficiency of the evaluator we could instead keep the association x = 4 in a separate structure called an *environment*, and evaluate the term (x * x) + x in that environment. A program that evaluates terms in this way is called an *interpreter*.

An environment is a function from variables to terms, with a finite domain. It is in essence the same thing as a substitution, but different notations are used. We write an environment as a list of pairs $x_1 = t_1, \ldots, x_n = t_n$, where the same variable x may occur several times and in that case the rightmost pair has priority. Thus, in the environment x = 3, y = 4, x = 5, z = 8 we only consider x = 5, not x = 3, which is said to be *hidden* by the pair x = 5. Finally, if e is an environment and x = t a pair, we denote by e, x = t the list obtained by extending e with the pair x = t.

During the evaluation of a term we might reach a free variable x. In this case, we will look for the term associated to this variable in the environment. It can be shown that, if we start with a closed term, then each time we reach a variable we will find an associated term in the environment.

In fact, the situation is slightly more complicated, because in addition to the term u associated to the variable in the environment, we will also need to find the environment associated to u. A pair of a term and an environment is called a *thunk*. We will write it ⟨u, e⟩.

Similarly, when we interpret a term of the form fun x -> t in an environment e, the result cannot simply be the term fun x -> t, because it might contain free variables and when interpreting the term t we will need the thunks associated to these variables in e. We introduce then a new notion of value, called a

G. Dowek, J.-J. Lévy, *Introduction to the Theory of Programming Languages*,
Undergraduate Topics in Computer Science,
DOI 10.1007/978-0-85729-076-2_3, © Springer-Verlag London Limited 2011

closure, consisting of a term *that must be of the form* fun x -> t and an environment e. We will write such values as follows ⟨x, t, e⟩. Values are no longer a subset of terms, and we will have to define a language of values independently from the language of terms.

As a consequence, we will need to rewrite the rules for the call by name bigstep operational semantics of PCF, in order to consider a relation of the form e ⊢ t ↪ V, read "t is interpreted as V in e ", where e is an environment, t a term and V a value. When the environment e is empty, this relation will be written ⊢ t ↪ V. The rules that extend the environment are the application rule, which adds a pair consisting of a variable x and a thunk ⟨u, e⟩, the let rule, which adds a pair consisting of the variable x and the thunk ⟨t, e⟩ and the fix rule, which adds a pair consisting of the variable x and the thunk ⟨fix x t, e⟩. In the latter rule, the term t is duplicated: one of the copies is interpreted and the other is kept in the environment for any recursive calls arising from the interpretation of the first one.

$$\frac{e' \vdash t \hookrightarrow V}{e \vdash x \hookrightarrow V} \text{ if e contains } x = \langle t, e' \rangle$$

$$\frac{e \vdash t \hookrightarrow \langle x, t', e' \rangle \qquad (e', x = \langle u, e \rangle) \vdash t' \hookrightarrow V}{e \vdash t\ u \hookrightarrow V}$$

$$\frac{}{e \vdash \text{fun } x \rightarrow t \hookrightarrow \langle x, t, e \rangle}$$

$$\frac{}{e \vdash n \hookrightarrow n}$$

$$\frac{e \vdash u \hookrightarrow q \qquad e \vdash t \hookrightarrow p}{e \vdash t \otimes u \hookrightarrow n} \text{ if } p \otimes q = n$$

$$\frac{e \vdash t \hookrightarrow 0 \qquad e \vdash u \hookrightarrow V}{e \vdash \text{ifz } t \text{ then } u \text{ else } v \hookrightarrow V}$$

$$\frac{e \vdash t \hookrightarrow n \qquad e \vdash v \hookrightarrow V}{e \vdash \text{ifz } t \text{ then } u \text{ else } v \hookrightarrow V} \begin{array}{l} \text{if } n \text{ is a} \\ \text{number} \neq 0 \end{array}$$

$$\frac{(e, x = \langle \text{fix } x\ t, e \rangle) \vdash t \hookrightarrow V}{e \vdash \text{fix } x\ t \hookrightarrow V}$$

$$\frac{(e, x = \langle t, e \rangle) \vdash u \hookrightarrow V}{e \vdash \text{let } x = t \text{ in } u \hookrightarrow V}$$

Exercise 3.1 Write a call by name interpreter for PCF.

Exercise 3.2 Which values will be obtained for the following terms according to the interpretation rules given above for PCF?

(fun x -> fun x -> x) 2 3

and

```
(fun x -> fun y -> ((fun x -> (x + y)) x)) 5 4
```

Compare with Exercises 2.7 and 2.13.

Exercise 3.3 Will the interpretation rules for PCF compute the value 10 or the value 11 for the term

```
let x = 4 in let f = fun y -> y + x
in let x = 5 in f 6?
```

Compare with Exercises 2.8 and 2.14.

3.2 Call by Value

The situation is simpler with a call by value semantics. Indeed, when interpreting a term of the form (fun x -> t) u, we start by interpreting the term u. The result is a value, that is, a number or a closure, and it suffices to bind the variable x to this value in the environment. Similarly, to interpret a term of the form let x = t in u, we start by interpreting the term t. The result is a value and it suffices to bind the variable x to this value in the environment. Thus, the environments will associate to variables values instead of thunks (which are suspended until they can be interpreted). We no longer need the notion of a thunk.

However, the evaluation rule for fix, unlike the application rule or the let rule, requires a variable to be substituted by a term of the form fix x t, which is not a value, and to evaluate such a term before substituting it or before storing it in the environment will give rise to infinite computations (as mentioned above). The environment will have to include then *extended values*, which are either values or thunks containing a term of the form fix x t and an environment e. When we access such an extended value, we will need to interpret it if it is a thunk. This leads us to the following rules

$$\frac{}{e \vdash x \hookrightarrow V} \ \text{if e contains } x = V$$

$$\frac{e' \vdash \text{fix } y\ t \hookrightarrow V}{e \vdash x \hookrightarrow V} \quad \begin{array}{l} \text{if e contains} \\ x = \langle \text{fix } y\ t, e' \rangle \end{array}$$

$$\frac{e \vdash u \hookrightarrow W \qquad e \vdash t \hookrightarrow \langle x,\ t',\ e' \rangle \qquad (e',\ x = W) \vdash t' \hookrightarrow V}{e \vdash t\ u \hookrightarrow V}$$

$$\frac{}{e \vdash \text{fun } x \rightarrow t \hookrightarrow \langle x,\ t,\ e \rangle}$$

$$\frac{}{e \vdash n \hookrightarrow n}$$

$$\frac{e \vdash u \hookrightarrow q \qquad e \vdash t \hookrightarrow p}{e \vdash t \otimes u \hookrightarrow n} \ \text{if } p \otimes q = n$$

$$\frac{e \vdash t \hookrightarrow 0 \qquad e \vdash u \hookrightarrow V}{e \vdash \text{ifz } t \text{ then } u \text{ else } v \hookrightarrow V}$$

$$\frac{e \vdash t \hookrightarrow n \qquad e \vdash v \hookrightarrow V}{e \vdash \text{ifz } t \text{ then } u \text{ else } v \hookrightarrow V} \quad \begin{array}{l} \text{if } n \text{ is a} \\ \text{number} \neq 0 \end{array}$$

$$\frac{(e, \ x = \langle \text{fix } x \ t, \ e \rangle) \vdash t \hookrightarrow V}{e \vdash \text{fix } x \ t \hookrightarrow V}$$

$$\frac{e \vdash t \hookrightarrow W \qquad (e, \ x = W) \vdash u \hookrightarrow V}{e \vdash \text{let } x = t \text{ in } u \hookrightarrow V}$$

Exercise 3.4 When we compute the value of the term (fact 3) where the function fact is defined by fix f fun n -> ifz n then 1 else n * (f (n - 1)), we start by calling recursively the function fact with argument 2, which will create an association between the variable n and the value 2. When we come back from the recursive call to compute the value of n and perform the multiplication, is the variable n associated to the value 2 or the value 3? Why?

Exercise 3.5 Write a call by value interpreter for PCF.

3.3 An Optimisation: de Bruijn Indices

In the big-step operational semantic rules, environments are lists of pairs consisting of a variable and an extended value. We could replace this structure by a pair of lists of the same length, one containing the variables and the other the values. Thus, the list x = 12, y = 14, z = 16, w = 18 could be replaced by the list of variables x, y, z, w and the list of extended values 12, 14, 16, 18. To find the extended value associated to a variable, we just need to search through the first list to find the variable's position, and then find in the other list the element at the same position. The position of a variable in the first list is a number, called the *de Bruijn index* of the variable in the environment. In general, we can associate the number 0 to the last element of the list—the rightmost element—, 1 to the previous, ..., n - 1 to the first element of the list—the leftmost one.

The list of variables which will be needed for the interpretation of each subterm can be computed before starting the process of interpretation. In fact, we can associate a de Bruijn index to each occurrence of a variable before interpreting the term. For example, if we interpret the term fun x -> fun y -> (x + (fun z -> fun w -> (x + y + z + w)) (2 * 8) (14 + 4)) (5 + 7) (20 - 6) the variable y will necessarily be interpreted in an environment of the form x = ., y = ., z = ., w = ., that is, to find the value associated to y we need to find the value with index 2. We can then associate this index to the variable from the start.

To compute the de Bruijn indices of the variables we simply need to traverse the term maintaining a *variable environment*, that is, a list of variables, where we associate the index p to the variable x in the environment e, if p is the position of the variable x in the environment e, starting from the end.

- $|x|_e = x^p$ where p is the position of x in the environment e
- $|t\ u|_e = |t|_e\ |u|_e$
- $|\text{fun}\ x\ \text{->}\ t|_e = \text{fun}\ x\ \text{->}\ |t|_{e,x}$
- $|n|_e = n$
- $|t\ \text{+}\ u|_e = |t|_e\ \text{+}\ |u|_e$
- $|t\ \text{-}\ u|_e = |t|_e\ \text{-}\ |u|_e$
- $|t\ \text{*}\ u|_e = |t|_e\ \text{*}\ |u|_e$
- $|t\ \text{/}\ u|_e = |t|_e\ \text{/}\ |u|_e$
- $|\text{ifz}\ t\ \text{then}\ u\ \text{else}\ v|_e = \text{ifz}\ |t|_e\ \text{then}\ |u|_e\ \text{else}\ |v|_e$
- $|\text{fix}\ x\ t|_e = \text{fix}\ x\ |t|_{e,x}$
- $|\text{let}\ x\ \text{=}\ t\ \text{in}\ u|_e = \text{let}\ x\ \text{=}\ |t|_e\ \text{in}\ |u|_{e,x}$

For example, the term above will be written `fun x -> fun y -> (x`^{1}` + (fun z -> fun w -> (x`^{3}` + y`^{2}` + z`^{1}` + w`^{0}`)) (2 * 8) (14 + 4)) (5 + 7) (20 - 6)`.

It is easy to show that an occurrence of a subterm translated in the variable environment $x_1, \ldots, x_n$ will always be interpreted in an environment of the form $x_1 = ., \ldots, x_n = .$. For this reason, to find the value of the variable associated to the index p we will just look for the pth element in the environment.

This suggests an alternative way to interpret a term: we start by computing the de Bruijn index for each occurrence of a variable; once the indices are known, we no longer need to keep in the environment the list of variables. The environment will simply be a list of extended values. Similarly, we can dispose of variable names in closures and in thunks. Indeed, variable names are useless now and we could for instance rewrite the term above as follows: `fun _ -> fun _ -> (_`^{1}` + (fun _ -> fun _ -> (_`^{3}` + _`^{2}` + _`^{1}` + _`^{0}`)) (2 * 8) (14 + 4)) (5 + 7) (20 - 6)`.

The big-step operational semantic rules can now be defined as follows

$$\frac{}{e \vdash \_^p \hookrightarrow V} \text{ if } V \text{ is the } p\text{th element of } e$$

$$\frac{e' \vdash \text{fix}\ \_\ t \hookrightarrow V}{e \vdash \_^p \hookrightarrow V} \quad \begin{array}{l} \text{if the } p\text{th element of } e \\ \text{is } \langle \text{fix}\ \_\ t, e' \rangle \end{array}$$

$$\frac{e \vdash u \hookrightarrow W \quad e \vdash t \hookrightarrow \langle t', e' \rangle \quad (e', W) \vdash t' \hookrightarrow V}{e \vdash t\ u \hookrightarrow V}$$

$$\frac{}{e \vdash \text{fun}\ \_\ \text{->}\ t \hookrightarrow \langle t, e \rangle}$$

$$\frac{}{e \vdash n \hookrightarrow n}$$

$$\frac{e \vdash u \hookrightarrow q \quad e \vdash t \hookrightarrow p}{e \vdash t \otimes u \hookrightarrow n} \text{ if } p \otimes q = n$$

$$\frac{e \vdash t \hookrightarrow 0 \qquad e \vdash u \hookrightarrow V}{e \vdash \texttt{ifz } t \texttt{ then } u \texttt{ else } v \hookrightarrow V}$$

$$\frac{e \vdash t \hookrightarrow n \qquad e \vdash v \hookrightarrow V}{e \vdash \texttt{ifz } t \texttt{ then } u \texttt{ else } v \hookrightarrow V} \quad \begin{array}{l} \text{if } n \text{ is a} \\ \text{number} \neq 0 \end{array}$$

$$\frac{(e, \ \langle \texttt{fix \_ } t, \ e \rangle) \vdash t \hookrightarrow V}{e \vdash \texttt{fix \_ } t \hookrightarrow V}$$

$$\frac{e \vdash t \hookrightarrow W \qquad (e, \ W) \vdash u \hookrightarrow V}{e \vdash \texttt{let \_ } = t \texttt{ in } u \hookrightarrow V}$$

Exercise 3.6 Write a program to replace each variable by its De Bruijn index. Write an interpreter for this language.

Exercise 3.7 Write the rules of the call by name big-step operational semantics using de Bruijn indices.

We will highlight the advantages of this notation, which eliminates the names of variables, when we study compilation in the next chapter.

In the meantime, notice that two terms have the same de Bruijn translations if and only if they are α-equivalent. This gives us a new definition of alphabetical equivalence. Replacing variables by indices that indicate the position where they are bound can be seen as a radical point of view that highlights the fact that bound variables are "dummies".

3.4 Construction of Functions via Fixed Points

In most programming languages, only functions can be recursively defined. The `fix` construct applies to a term of the form `fun`, or we could also replace the symbol `fix` by a symbol `fixfun f x -> t` that binds two variables in its argument. The call by value big-step semantic rule for the latter can be derived from the rules given above for `fix` and `fun`

$$\overline{e \vdash \texttt{fixfun f x -> } t \hookrightarrow \langle x, \ t, \ (e, \ f = \langle \texttt{fixfun f x -> } t, \ e \rangle) \rangle}$$

In this case, we could define simpler variations of the rules for the call by value interpreter.

3.4.1 First Variation: Recursive Closures

We will distinguish closures of the form $\langle x, \ t, \ (e, \ f = \langle \texttt{fixfun f x -> } t, \ e \rangle) \rangle$, which we will write $\langle f, \ x, \ t, \ e \rangle$ and call *recursive closures*.

The rule that we have given to interpret the construction `fixfun f x -> t` can be reformulated as follows

$$\frac{}{\text{e} \vdash \text{fixfun f x -> t} \hookrightarrow \langle\text{f, x, t, e}\rangle}$$

When we interpret an application `t u` under a call by value semantics, if the term `t` is interpreted as the recursive closure $\langle\text{f, x, t', e'}\rangle$, that is, $\langle\text{x, t',}$ $\text{(e', f} = \langle\text{fixfun f x -> t', e'}\rangle)\rangle$ and the term `u` as the value `W`, then to interpret the term `t u`, the application rule requires to interpret the term `t'` in the environment `e', f` = $\langle\text{fixfun f x -> t', e'}\rangle$, `x = W`.

We can anticipate the interpretation of the thunk $\langle\text{fixfun f x -> t', e}\rangle$ that appears in this environment, and this gives rise to the rule `fixfun`, the recursive closure $\langle\text{f, x, t', e'}\rangle$. In the case of recursive closures, the application rule can then be specialised as follows

$$\frac{\text{e} \vdash \text{u} \hookrightarrow \text{W} \qquad \text{e} \vdash \text{t} \hookrightarrow \langle\text{f, x, t', e'}\rangle \qquad (\text{e', f} = \langle\text{f, x, t', e'}\rangle, \text{x} = \text{W}) \vdash \text{t'} \hookrightarrow \text{V}}{\text{e} \vdash \text{t u} \hookrightarrow \text{V}}$$

Thunks are no longer used in this rule; thus, under call by value, by introducing recursive closures we eliminate thunks and we no longer need the rule to interpret them.

A final simplification: standard closures $\langle\text{x, t, e}\rangle$ can be replaced by recursive closures $\langle\text{f, x, t, e}\rangle$ where `f` is an arbitrary variable that does not occur in `t`. We can then discard the application rule for the case of standard closures.

Finally, we obtain the rules

$$\frac{}{\text{e} \vdash \text{x} \hookrightarrow \text{V}} \text{ if e contains x = V}$$

$$\frac{\text{e} \vdash \text{u} \hookrightarrow \text{W} \qquad \text{e} \vdash \text{t} \hookrightarrow \langle\text{f, x, t', e'}\rangle \qquad (\text{e', f} = \langle\text{f, x, t', e'}\rangle, \text{x} = \text{W}) \vdash \text{t'} \hookrightarrow \text{V}}{\text{e} \vdash \text{t u} \hookrightarrow \text{V}}$$

$$\frac{}{\text{e} \vdash \text{fun x -> t} \hookrightarrow \langle\text{f, x, t, e}\rangle}$$

where `f` is an arbitrary variable, different from `x`, that does not occur in `t` or `e`

$$\frac{}{\text{e} \vdash \text{fixfun f x -> t} \hookrightarrow \langle\text{f, x, t, e}\rangle}$$

$$\frac{}{\text{e} \vdash \text{n} \hookrightarrow \text{n}}$$

$$\frac{\text{e} \vdash \text{u} \hookrightarrow \text{q} \qquad \text{e} \vdash \text{t} \hookrightarrow \text{p}}{\text{e} \vdash \text{t} \otimes \text{u} \hookrightarrow \text{n}} \text{ if } \text{p} \otimes \text{q} = \text{n}$$

$$\frac{e \vdash t \hookrightarrow 0 \qquad e \vdash u \hookrightarrow V}{e \vdash \text{ifz } t \text{ then } u \text{ else } v \hookrightarrow V}$$

$$\frac{e \vdash t \hookrightarrow n \qquad e \vdash v \hookrightarrow V}{e \vdash \text{ifz } t \text{ then } u \text{ else } v \hookrightarrow V} \begin{array}{l} \text{if } n \text{ is a} \\ \text{number} \neq 0 \end{array}$$

$$\frac{e \vdash t \hookrightarrow W \qquad (e, \ x = W) \vdash u \hookrightarrow V}{e \vdash \text{let } x = t \text{ in } u \hookrightarrow V}$$

Exercise 3.8 Write a call by value interpreter for PCF, using recursive closures.

Exercise 3.9 How will the rules of the big-step operational semantics with recursive closures change if variables are replaced by de Bruijn indices—see Sect. 3.3?

3.4.2 Second Variation: Rational Values

In the rule

$$e \vdash \text{fixfun } f \ x \ \text{-> } t \hookrightarrow \langle x, \ t, \ (e, \ f = \langle \text{fixfun } f \ x \ \text{-> } t, \ e \rangle) \rangle$$

we can anticipate the interpretation of the thunk $\langle \text{fixfun } f \ x \ \text{-> } t, \ e \rangle$. Of course, the value of this thunk is the term $\langle x, \ t, \ (e, \ f = \langle \text{fixfun } f \ x \ \text{-> } t, \ e \rangle) \rangle$ where the thunk occurs again. We could decide to interpret it again, and again. ...

   As previously said, this kind of interpretation of a term of the form fix f t before substituting it or storing it in the environment leads to an infinite computation. Here, it leads to the construction of the infinite value $\langle x, \ t, \ (e, \ f = \langle x, \ t, \ (e, \ f = \langle x, \ t, \ (e, \ f = \langle x, \ t, \ (e, \ f = \dots) \rangle) \rangle) \rangle) \rangle$, which is an infinite term, but a rational one. There are well-known techniques for the representation of rational trees in the computer's memory. Here, we could represent this value by the structure.

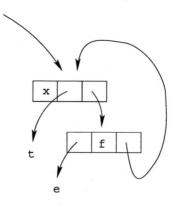

Using the notation `FIX X ⟨x, t, (e, f = X)⟩` for this rational value, we can replace the rule above by

$$\overline{e \vdash \texttt{fixfun f x -> t} \hookrightarrow \texttt{FIX X ⟨x, t, (e, f = X)⟩}}$$

and again thunks will no longer be needed.

Note that it is sometimes better to represent such rational value in an equivalent way

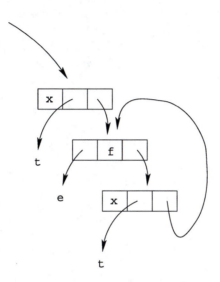

and in this case we could instead define rational environments.

Exercise 3.10 Write a call by value interpreter for PCF using rational values.

Exercise 3.11 How do these big-step operational semantic rules change if we replace variables by their de Bruijn indices—see Sect. 3.3?

Exercise 3.12 Could the technique of rational values be used to design an interpreter for the full PCF, that is, where we could define via fixed points not only functions but also arbitrary objects? Hint: what is the rational representation of the value of the term `fix x x`?

To summarise, in this section we have seen that if a variable x has an occurrence in the term t, the reduction rule `fix x t ⟶ (fix x t/x)t` can be applied an infinite number of times starting from the term `fix x t`, because the term `(fix x t/x)t` contains again the term `fix x t` as a subterm. This corresponds to the replacement, in a recursive definition `f = G(f)`, of f by `G(f)` an infinite number of times, which leads to the infinite program `f = G(G(G(...)))`. In a sense, this explains the intuition that recursive programs are infinite programs. For example, the term `fact` could be written `fun x -> ifz x then 1 else x * (ifz x - 1 then 1 else (x - 1) * (ifz x - 2 then 1 else (x - 2) * ···))`. This replacement must only be done on demand: in a lazy way.

We have seen that there are several ways to express this behaviour in the semantics of PCF—and finally in the code of a PCF interpreter: substitute x by `fix x t` and freeze this redex if it is under a `fun` or an `ifz`, store this redex as a thunk or a recursive closure and "unfreeze" the thunk on demand, represent the term `f = G(G(G(...)))` as a rational tree and traverse it on demand. A final method could be to use the encoding of `fix` given in Exercise 2.10, and only reduce this term (which requires the duplication of a subterm) when needed.

Exercise 3.13 (An extension of PCF with pairs) We extend PCF with the following constructions: `t,u` represents the pair where the first component is `t` and the second is `u`; `fst t` and `snd t` are, respectively, the first and second component of the pair `t`. Write small-step and big-step operational semantic rules for this extension of PCF. Write an interpreter for this extension of PCF.

Exercise 3.14 (An extension of PCF with lists) We extend PCF with the following constructions: `nil` denotes the empty list, `cons n l` denotes a list where the first element is the natural number n and l is the rest of the list, `ifnil t then u else v` checks whether a list is empty or not, `hd l` returns the first element of the list l and `tl l` the list l without its first element. Write small-step and big-step operational semantic rules for this extension of PCF. Write an interpreter for this extension of PCF. Write a program to implement a sorting algorithm over these lists.

Exercise 3.15 (An extension of PCF with trees) We extend PCF with the following constructions: `L n` denotes a tree that consists of one leaf labelled by the natural number n, `N t u` denotes a tree with two subtrees t and u, `ifleaf t then u else v` checks whether its first argument is a tree of the form `L n` or `N t u`, `content t` denotes the content of the tree t if it is a leaf, `left t` and `right t` denote, respectively, the left and right subtrees of t if it is not a leaf. Write small-step and big-step operational semantic rules for this extension of PCF. Write an interpreter for this extension of PCF.

Chapter 4
Compilation

When a computer comes out of the factory, it is not capable of interpreting a PCF term, not even a Caml or Java program. For a computer to be able to run a PCF, Caml or Java program, we need to have an interpreter for the language, which must be written in the machine language of the computer. In the previous chapter we described the principles underlying PCF interpretation, and we wrote an interpreter in a high-level language, such as Caml. We could continue this line of thought, and try to write now an interpreter in machine language. . . .

One possibility is to leave the realm of interpretation and move towards a *compiler*. An interpreter takes a PCF term as input and returns its value. A compiler, instead, is a program that takes a PCF term as argument and returns a program, in machine language, whose execution returns the value of the term. In other words, a PCF compiler is a program that translates PCF terms into machine language, that is, into a language which can be directly executed by the machine.

One of the advantages of using a compiler is that the program is translated once and for all, when it is compiled, rather than each time it is executed. Once compiled, the execution is usually faster. Another advantage comes from the fact that a compiler can compile itself, we call this *bootstrapping* (see Exercise 4.4), whereas an interpreter cannot interpret itself.

The implementation of a compiler should be guided by the rules of the operational semantics of the language (as was the case for the interpreter). To simplify, we will focus on a fragment of PCF where only functions can be defined recursively, and we will use the big-step semantics with recursive closures—see Sect. 3.4.

The machine language that we will use is not a commercial one: it is the machine language of an imaginary computer. This kind of machine is called an *abstract machine*. We will write a program that will simulate the behaviour of this machine. The use of an abstract machine is not only motivated by pedagogical reasons, there are practical reasons too: the main compilers for Caml and Java, for instance, use abstract machines. Compiled programs are executed by a program that simulates the workings of the abstract machine, or are further translated (in a second compilation phase) to the machine language of a concrete machine.

G. Dowek, J.-J. Lévy, *Introduction to the Theory of Programming Languages*,
Undergraduate Topics in Computer Science,
DOI 10.1007/978-0-85729-076-2_4, © Springer-Verlag London Limited 2011

4.1 An Interpreter Written in a Language Without Functions

In Chap. 2, we gave a big-step operational semantics for PCF and we used it to derive an interpreter for this language. For example, the rule

$$\frac{e \vdash u \hookrightarrow q \qquad e \vdash t \hookrightarrow p}{e \vdash t + u \hookrightarrow n} \text{ if } p + q = n$$

results in the following piece of Caml code for the PCF interpreter

```
let rec interp env p = match p with
| Plus(t,u) ->
    let w = interp env u
    in let v = interp env t
        in (match (v,w) with | (Const(n), Const(m)) ->
                                   Const(n + m)
                             | ...)
| ...
```

Since Caml allows us to write local definitions, we can compute the value of the term `interp env t` and recover the value w after the computation, even if the variable w is bound to other values during the computation.

   If we tried to write the interpreter in machine language, or in any language that does not permit local definitions, then we would need to devise a mechanism to memorise the value w, for example using a stack: we could interpret the term u, put the result in the stack, then interpret the term t and finally pop the top of the stack and add it to the result of the interpretation.

   In this way, to interpret the term $((((1 + 2) + 3) + 4) + 5) + 6$ we need to put the number 6, then the number 5, ..., then the number 2 in the stack, then pop the number on the top of the stack (that is, 2) and add it to the number 1, then pop the number 3 and add it to the previous result, then... pop the number 6 and add it to the previous result, to obtain the final result: 21.

4.2 From Interpretation to Compilation

This interpreter can be decomposed into two programs. The first one can be seen as an object with two fields: a field that contains a natural number and that we call an *accumulator*, and a field that contains a list of natural numbers, called the *stack*. We have the following operations

- **Ldi** n: puts the number n in the accumulator,
- **Push**: puts the contents of the accumulator on the top of the stack,
- **Add**: adds the top of the stack and the accumulator, leaves the result in the accumulator, and pops the top of the stack.

This object is our abstract machine, and the three instructions above constitute its machine language. The fields are called *registers*.

The second program takes a PCF term as input and, depending on the term, produces machine instructions, which will be executed by the machine, one by one. If t is a PCF term, we denote by |t| the sequence of abstract machine instructions generated by this program during the interpretation of the term. For instance, for the term ((((1 + 2) + 3) + 4) + 5) + 6, the machine instructions generated are: **Ldi** 6, **Push**, **Ldi** 5, **Push**, **Ldi** 4, **Push**, **Ldi** 3, **Push**, **Ldi** 2, **Push**, **Ldi** 1, **Add**, **Add**, **Add**, **Add**, **Add**.

Exercise 4.1 Which instructions will be executed by the abstract machine when interpreting the term 1 + (2 + (3 + (4 + (5 + 6))))?

This way of sharing the work resembles the behaviour of a car driver and a passenger in an unfamiliar city: the passenger reads the map and gives instructions to the driver, who follows the instructions without really knowing where the car is.

If the passenger could generate the instructions just by looking at the map, it would be possible to record the list of instructions in a compact disk, which the driver could then listen to in the car. In this scenario, the passenger does not need to be in the car to guide the driver. Similarly, the interpreter could leave the sequence |t| of instructions in a file, and the file could then be executed later by the abstract machine. We have just transformed the interpreter into a compiler.

In general, we consider that the abstract machine contains, in addition to the accumulator and the stack, a third register: the *code*, the list of instructions that have to be executed. At the beginning, the abstract machine looks for an instruction in the code register, executes it, then looks for another instruction... until the code register becomes empty. As we will see, the fact that the execution of an instruction may add new instructions to the code register will allow us to write loops and recursive definitions.

4.3 An Abstract Machine for PCF

4.3.1 The Environment

So far we have only compiled a fragment of PCF: numbers and addition. Can this principle be generalised to the full language?

First, recall that in PCF a term has to be interpreted in an environment. In addition to the accumulator, stack, and code, our abstract machine needs a fourth register: *the environment*. The machine must also include an instruction **Extend** x to extend the environment, adding the definition x = V where V is the content of the accumulator, and an instruction **Search** x to look for the value associated to x in the environment and put it in the accumulator.

When the machine executes the code generated by the compilation of several nested applications, the environment will change several times, and at the end of the execution the initial environment should be restored. The abstract machine needs then instructions **Pushenv** and **Popenv** to put the contents of the environment in the stack and recover it. These operations are often further decomposed into several operations to push and pop individual elements of the environment, but here we will not decompose them in this way.

4.3.2 Closures

In PCF it is also necessary to define closures as values. In addition to the instruction **Ldi** n, we will need an instruction **Mkclos**(f,x,t), with two variables f and x and a term t as arguments. This instruction will build the closure ⟨f, x, t, e⟩, where e is the content of the environment register, and put the closure in the accumulator.

4.3.3 PCF Constructs

It is not difficult to compile a term of the form fun x -> t or fixfun f x -> t since we can simply generate the instruction **Mkclos**(f,x,t) to build a closure, which is the value of this kind of term.

In the same way, it is easy to compile a term of the form x, we just need to generate the instruction **Search** x to look for the value associated to x in the environment.

Let us consider now the compilation of a term of the form t u. The corresponding big-step semantics rule is

$$\frac{e \vdash u \hookrightarrow W \qquad e \vdash t \hookrightarrow \langle f, x, t', e' \rangle \qquad (e', f = \langle f, x, t', e' \rangle, x = W) \vdash t' \hookrightarrow V}{e \vdash t\ u \hookrightarrow V}$$

To interpret the term t u in the environment e, we start by interpreting u in the environment e, which returns the value W. We then interpret the term t in the environment e, obtaining the closure ⟨f, x, t', e'⟩, and finally we interpret t' in the environment (e', f = ⟨f, x, t', e'⟩), x = W, to obtain the final result.

Now, let us see how an interpreter running in an abstract machine will deal with that term: to interpret the term t u, the abstract machine starts by interpreting u, and puts the result in the stack. Then, it interprets the term t, resulting in the closure ⟨f, x, t', e'⟩, and puts in the environment register the environment e', f = ⟨f, x, t', e'⟩, x = W, where W is the value at the top of the stack, which will then be removed from the stack. Finally, the machine interprets the term t'. To ensure that the contents of the environment register are restored at the end of the operations, it should be put in the stack at the beginning of the interpretation, and recovered from the stack at the end.

Let us consider now the compilation process for such a term. The interpretation of the term u is replaced by the execution of the sequence |u| of instructions, and similarly the interpretation of the term t is replaced by the execution of the sequence |t| of instructions. The interpretation of t′ has to be replaced by the execution of the sequence |t′| of instructions. However, there is a difficulty here: t′ is not a subterm of t u, it is provided by the closure resulting from the interpretation of t. We then need to modify the notion of closure, and replace the term t in ⟨f, x, t, e⟩ by a sequence i of instructions. Thus, terms of the form fun x -> t and fixfun f x -> t should not be compiled into **Mkclos**(f, x, t), instead, they should be compiled into **Mkclos**(f, x, |t|) to build the closure ⟨f, x, |t|, e⟩ where e is the content of the environment register.

Finally, we need to include in the machine an instruction **Apply** that takes a closure ⟨f, x, i, e⟩ from the accumulator, puts the environment e, f = ⟨f, x, i, e⟩, x = W, where W is the top of the stack, in the environment register, discards the top of the stack and adds to the code register the sequence i of instructions.

The term t u can then be compiled as the sequence of instructions **Pushenv**, |u|, **Push**, |t|, **Apply**, **Popenv**.

Summarising, the abstract machine has the set of instructions **Ldi** n, **Push**, **Add**, **Extend** x, **Search** x, **Pushenv**, **Popenv**, **Mkclos**(f,x,i) and **Apply**. To complete it, we just need to add the arithmetic operations **Sub**, **Mult**, **Div** and the test **Test**(i,j) to compile the operators -, *, / and ifz.

4.3.4 Using de Bruijn Indices

To simplify the machine we can use De Bruijn indices—see Sect. 3.3. Recall that the instruction **Search** x is generated by the compilation of variables, and we have already seen that it is possible to determine the index of each variable occurrence statically. We could then compile a variable x using the instruction **Search** n, where n is a number, instead of **earch** x.

De Bruijn indices can be computed at the same time as the compilation is performed, it suffices to compile a term in a variable environment, and compile the variable x in the environment e by the instruction **Search** n, where n is the position of the variable x in the environment e, starting by the end.

This mechanism allows us to dispose of variables in environments, closures, and instructions **Mkclos** and **Extend**. Our abstract machine includes the instructions **Ldi** n, **Push**, **Extend**, **Search** n, **Pushenv**, **Popenv**, **Mkclos** i, **Apply**, **Test**(i,j), **Add**, **Sub**, **Mult** and **Div**.

4.3.5 Small-Step Operational Semantics

The machine state, the contents of its registers, is a tuple consisting of a value (the accumulator), a list where each element is either a value or a list of values (the stack), a list of values (the environment), and a sequence of instructions (the code).

A small execution step consists of getting an instruction from the code register and executing it. The small-step semantics of the machine can be easily defined:

- (a,s,e,((**Mkclos** i),c)) $\longrightarrow$ (⟨i,e⟩,s,e,c)
- (a,s,e,(**Push**,c)) $\longrightarrow$ (a,(a,s),e,c)
- (a,s,e,(**Extend**,c)) $\longrightarrow$ (a,s,(e,a),c)
- (a,s,e,((**Search** n),c)) $\longrightarrow$ (V,s,e,c) if V is the nth value in e (starting from the end)
- (a,s,e,(**Pushenv**,c)) $\longrightarrow$ (a,(e,s),e,c)
- (a,(e',s),e,(**Popenv**,c)) $\longrightarrow$ (a,s,e',c)
- (⟨i,e'⟩,(W,s),e,(**Apply**,c)) $\longrightarrow$ (⟨i,e'⟩,s,(e', ⟨i,e'⟩, W), i c)
- (a,s,e,((**Ldi** n),c)) $\longrightarrow$ (n,s,e,c)
- (n,(m,s),e,(**Add**,c)) $\longrightarrow$ (n + m,s,e,c)
- (n,(m,s),e,(**Sub**,c)) $\longrightarrow$ (n - m,s,e,c)
- (n,(m,s),e,(**Mult**,c)) $\longrightarrow$ (n * m,s,e,c)
- (n,(m,s),e,(**Div**,c)) $\longrightarrow$ (n / m,s,e,c)
- (0,s,e,((**Test**(i,j)),c)) $\longrightarrow$ (0,s,e,i c)
- (n,s,e,((**Test**(i,j)),c)) $\longrightarrow$ (n,s,e,j c) if n is a number different from 0

An irreducible term is a tuple where the fourth component—the contents of the code register—is empty. If i is a sequence of instructions and if the term (0,[ ],[ ],i) reduces to an irreducible term of the form (V,_,_,[ ]), then we say that V is the result of the execution of i, and we write i $\Rightarrow$ V.

4.4 Compilation of PCF

We can now give the compilation rules for PCF

- $|x|_e$ = **Search** n where n is the position of x in the environment e
- $|t \ u|_e$ = **Pushenv**, $|u|_e$, **Push**, $|t|_e$, **Apply**, **Popenv**
- $|fun \ x \rightarrow t|_e$ = **Mkclos** $|t|_{e,\_,x}$
- $|fixfun \ f \ x \rightarrow t|_e$ = **Mkclos** $|t|_{e, f, x}$
- $|n|_e$ = **Ldi** n
- $|t + u|_e$ = $|u|_e$, **Push**, $|t|_e$, **Add**
- $|t - u|_e$ = $|u|_e$, **Push**, $|t|_e$, **Sub**
- $|t * u|_e$ = $|u|_e$, **Push**, $|t|_e$, **Mult**
- $|t / u|_e$ = $|u|_e$, **Push**, $|t|_e$, **Div**
- $|ifz \ t \ then \ u \ else \ v|_e$ = $|t|_e$, **Test**($|u|_e$,$|v|_e$)

– $|$let x = t in u$|_e$ = **Pushenv,** $|$t$|_e$, **Extend,** $|$u$|_{e, x}$, **Popenv**

For example, the compilation of

```
let f = fixfun f x ->(ifz x then 1 else
                         (x * (f (x - 1))))  in f 6
```

generates the sequence of instructions **Pushenv, Mkclos [Search** 0, **Test([Ldi** 1], **[Pushenv, Ldi** 1, **Push, Search** 0, **Sub, Push, Search** 1, **Apply, Popenv, Push, Search** 0, **Mult])], Extend, Pushenv, Ldi** 6, **Push, Search** 0, **Apply, Popenv, Popenv** and the result of its execution is the number 720.

The correctness of the compilation, and of the semantics of the abstract machine, can be stated as follows: if V is a numeric value, then ⊢ t ↪ V if and only if $|$t$|$ ⇒ V.

Exercise 4.2 Write an abstract machine and a compiler for PCF.

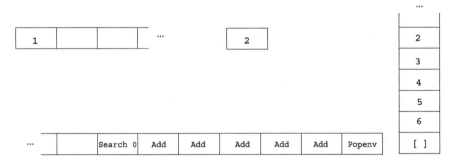

The state of the abstract machine at the beginning of the 14th execution step for the program **Pushenv, Ldi** 1, **Extend, Ldi** 6, **Push, Ldi** 5, **Push, Ldi** 4, **Push, Ldi** 3, **Push, Ldi** 2, **Push, Search** 0, **Add, Add, Add, Add, Add, Popenv.**

Exercise 4.3 We extend PCF with the tree operators described in Exercise 3.15. Write a compiler and an abstract machine for this extension of PCF.

Exercise 4.4 (A bootstrapping compiler) Many kinds of data structures can be represented using the trees described in Exercise 3.15. To start with, we can represent a natural number n as a tree L n. The character c can be represented by the tree L n where n is a code, for instance the ASCII code of the character c. If $t_1, t_2, \ldots, t_n$ are trees, the list $t_1, t_2, \ldots, t_n$ can be represented by the tree N(t_1, N(t_2, ..., N(t_n, L 0)...)). Finally, values of a type defined by constructors that are themselves representable could be defined by enumerating the constructors and representing the value C(V_1, V_2, ..., V_n) by the list L p, $t_1, t_2, \ldots, t_n$ where p is the number associated to the constructor C and $t_1, t_2, \ldots, t_n$ represent the values $V_1, V_2, \ldots, V_n$.

We could, in particular, represent in this way programs written in the extended PCF language, or in the language of the abstract machine in Exercise 4.3. Modify the compiler and the abstract machine in Exercise 4.3 to accept programs represented by binary trees. The abstract machine will take two inputs: a compiled program, represented by a tree, and a value, and will apply the program to the value.

Translate the compiler in Exercise 4.3 to PCF. After writing the compiler, compile it with the compiler defined in Exercise 4.3. The result is the first compiler executed by the PCF abstract machine. Compile this compiler (it will compile itself). Verify that the code produced is the same that was obtained with the compiler in Exercise 4.3. If this is true, we can destroy the first compiler and use instead the second: this is the bootstrap process.

Chapter 5
PCF with Types

In Chap. 2, we remarked that, in contrast with mathematical functions, the domain of PCF functions is not specified. For this reason, it is possible to apply the function `fun x -> x + 1` to the function `fun x -> x + 2`, even if this application is meaningless.

It is sometimes convenient to be able to apply any object to another object. For example, we can apply the identity function `fun x -> x` to itself, using the term `(fun x -> x) (fun x -> x)` that reduces to `fun x -> x`. More generally, the identity function in PCF is defined for any object, whereas in Mathematics it always has to be restricted to a specific domain. The ability to apply an object to itself was essential to show that the `fix` construct can be simulated in PCF using application and `fun`—see Exercise 2.10.

However, the unrestricted application of an object to another may rise a number of problems. For example, we saw that the terms `1 2, 1 + (fun x -> x), ifz (fun x -> x) then 1 else 2` were irreducible closed terms according to the small-step semantics of PCF, but they are not values.

The big-step operational semantics instead does not associate any result to a term such as `(fun x -> x) 1 2`. In practice, if we interpret a term of the form `t u` where `t` results in a number instead of a term of the form `fun`, an error is raised. This error will be detected at run time, instead of being detected statically (before execution) as one would expect.

The fact that the domain of a PCF function is not specified also makes it more difficult to give a denotational semantics for PCF.

The goal of this chapter is to define a version of PCF where functions come with associated domains, and to show that if a program is well-formed in this language, its interpretation cannot produce the errors mentioned above. We will also give a simple denotational semantics for this language.

5.1 Types

In Mathematics, the domain of a function is a set (any set). For example, we can define a function m from $2\mathbb{N}$ to $\mathbb{N}$ that associates to each even number its half. Then,

G. Dowek, J.-J. Lévy, *Introduction to the Theory of Programming Languages*,
Undergraduate Topics in Computer Science,
DOI 10.1007/978-0-85729-076-2_5, © Springer-Verlag London Limited 2011

to check whether the expression m (3 + (4 + 1)) is well-formed or not, that is, to check whether the argument is in the domain of the function, we need to check whether 3 + (4 + 1) is even or not. For arbitrary sets, the problem of deciding whether a given element belongs to the set is undecidable in general. Therefore, the problem of checking the validity of terms is also undecidable in general. Besides, to know whether a term such as ifz t then u else v will produce an error or not, we need to know whether the value of t is a natural number or a term of the form fun (the parity of the number is not relevant in this case).

These two remarks lead us to restrict the class of sets used to define the domains of functions. The sets in this restricted class will be called *types*.

5.1.1   PCF with Types

In PCF, types are inductively defined by

- nat—that is, $\mathbb{N}$—is a type,
- if A and B are types then A -> B—that is, the set of all the functions from A to B—is a type.

Types can then be defined using a language that includes the constant nat and the symbol -> with two arguments that do not bind any variables. Such a term is also called a *type*.

Functions in PCF were written fun x -> t, but will now include the type of the variable x. Thus, we will write fun x:nat -> x for the identity function on the natural number, and fun x:(nat -> nat) -> x for the identity function on functions from natural numbers to natural numbers. In general, the symbol fun will now have two arguments, a type and a term; it will bind a variable in the second argument. The typed version of the language PCF is a language with two sorts of objects: terms and types, and the arity of the symbol fun is ((type), (term, term), term). Also the symbols fix and let must now indicate the type of the bound variable.

Summarising, typed PCF includes

- a term symbol fun with a type argument and a term argument, which binds a variable in the second argument,
- a term symbol α with two term arguments, that does not bind any variable,
- an infinite number of term constants to represent the natural numbers,
- four term symbols +, -, * and /, each with two arguments which do not bind any variables in their arguments,
- a term symbol ifz with three term arguments which do not bind any variables,
- a term symbol fix with a type argument and a term argument, which binds a variable in the second argument,
- a term symbol let with three arguments, where the first is a type and the others terms, binding a variable in the third argument,
- a type constant nat,

– a type symbol -> with two type arguments and which does not bind any variable
  in its arguments.

Alternatively, we can define the syntax of the typed version of PCF inductively

```
A = X
  | nat
  | A -> A
t = x
  | fun x:A -> t
  | t t
  | n
  | t + t | t - t | t * t | t / t
  | ifz t then t else t
  | fix x:A t
  | let x:A = t in t
```

5.1.2 The Typing Relation

We can now define by induction the relation $t : A$, read "the term t has type A".
More precisely, we will define by induction a ternary relation $e \vdash t : A$, as we
did for the interpretation relation, where t is a term that might have free variables
and e is a *typing environment* that associates a type to each variable. This is an
inductive definition, similar to the inductive definition of PCF's big-step operational
semantics. We could imagine that it is the operational semantics of a language with
the same syntax as PCF but where the interpretation of a term returns a type instead
of a value—for this reason, it is called an *abstract interpretation* of the term.

$$\frac{}{e \vdash x : A} \text{ if } e \text{ contains } x : A$$

$$\frac{e \vdash u : A \quad e \vdash t : A \to B}{e \vdash t\, u : B}$$

$$\frac{(e,\ x : A) \vdash t : B}{e \vdash \text{fun } x{:}A \to t : A \to B}$$

$$\frac{}{e \vdash n : \text{nat}}$$

$$\frac{e \vdash u : \text{nat} \quad e \vdash t : \text{nat}}{e \vdash t \otimes u : \text{nat}}$$

$$\frac{e \vdash t : \text{nat} \quad e \vdash u : A \quad e \vdash v : A}{e \vdash \text{ifz } t \text{ then } u \text{ else } v : A}$$

$$\frac{(e,\ x : A) \vdash t : A}{e \vdash \text{fix } x{:}A\, t : A}$$

$$\frac{e \vdash t : A \qquad (e, \ x : A) \vdash u : B}{e \vdash \texttt{let } x{:}A \ = \ t \ \texttt{in } u \ : \ B}$$

In the first rule only the rightmost declaration for x is taken into account, the others are hidden.

The language includes variables of various sorts, in particular type variables for which we will use capital letters. Since no symbol can bind a type variable, a closed term will not contain type variables. Moreover, if a closed term t has the type A in the empty environment, then the type A must be closed too. So, type variables are not really used here; they will be used in the next chapter.

Let e be an environment and t a term. Reasoning by induction on t, we can show that the term t has at most one type in the environment e.

We can build a *type checking* algorithm based on the typing rules given above. The algorithm will check whether a term t has a type in an environment e, and if it does, it will give the type as a result. It will do this by typing recursively the direct subterms of the given term, and will then compute the type of term using the types of the subterms.

Exercise 5.1 Write a type checker for PCF.

Reduction is still confluent on the typed language, and types bring us an additional property: all the terms that do not contain the operator fix terminate— Tait's Theorem. It will be impossible to build a term such as (fun x -> (x x)) (fun x -> (x x)), which does not terminate and does not contain fix.

Exercise 5.2 Write typing rules for the version of PCF that uses de Bruijn indices instead of variable names—see Sect. 3.3.

Exercise 5.3 We extend PCF with the constructs described in Exercise 3.13 to define pairs, and we introduce a symbol × to denote the Cartesian product of two types. Write typing rules for this extension of PCF. Write a type-checker for this extension of PCF.

Exercise 5.4 We extend PCF with the constructs described in Exercise 3.14 to define lists, and we introduce a type natlist for these lists. Write typing rules for this extension of PCF. Write a type-checker for this extension of PCF.

Exercise 5.5 We extend PCF with the constructs described in Exercise 3.15 to define trees, and we introduce a type nattree for these trees. Write typing rules for this extension of PCF. Write a type-checker for this extension of PCF.

5.2 No Errors at Run Time

We will now show that the interpretation of a correctly typed term cannot produce a type error at run time. For this we can use the small-step or the big-step semantics; the proof is slightly different depending on the semantics we use.

5.2.1 Using Small-Step Operational Semantics

Using the small-step operational semantics of the language, the property can be formulated as follows: the result of the computation of a typed closed term, if it exists, is a value. In other words, a typed closed term evaluates to a natural number or a closed term of the form fun x -> t; it can never be a stuck term: $V_1\ V_2$, where V_1 and V_2 are irreducible closed terms and V_1 is not a term of the form fun x -> t, $V_1 \otimes V_2$, where V_1 and V_2 are irreducible closed terms which are not both numbers, or a term of the form ifz V_1 then V_2 else V_3 where V_1, V_2 and V_3 are irreducible closed terms and V_1 is not a number.

The first lemma, which we will not prove here, is usually called *subject reduction*. It says that if a closed term t of type A reduces in one step to the term u (t $\triangleright$ u), then u also has type A. We can deduce that if a closed term t of type A reduces to u in any number of steps (t $\triangleright^*$ u), then u also has type A.

The next step in the proof consists of showing that a term of the form fun cannot have the type nat and similarly a numeric constant cannot have a type of the form A -> B. This is done by a simple structural induction over the typing relation.

The proof proceeds by showing that an irreducible closed term t of type nat is a constant representing a natural number and an irreducible closed term t of type A -> B has the form fun. This is done by structural induction on t.

Since t is a closed term, it cannot be a variable. Since it is irreducible, it cannot be a fix or a let.

We show that t cannot be an application, an arithmetic operator or a conditional. If t is an application t = u v then u has a type of the form C -> D. By induction hypothesis, this term must be of the form fun, and therefore t is a redex, contradicting our assumption (t is irreducible). If t is an arithmetic operator t = u $\otimes$ v then u and v have type nat. By induction hypothesis, they are numeric constants and therefore t is a redex, contradicting our assumption (t is irreducible). If t is a term of the form t = ifz u then v else w then u has type nat. By induction hypothesis, u is a numeric constant and therefore t is a redex, contradicting our assumption (t is irreducible).

An irreducible closed term t is then either a numeric constant or a term of the form fun. If it has type nat, it is a constant; if it has type A -> B, it is a fun.

If a well-typed closed term can be reduced to an irreducible closed term, this irreducible term will also be well typed, and will therefore be either a numeric constant or a term of the form fun.

5.2.2 Using Big-Step Operational Semantics

The property is formulated differently using the big-step operational semantics of the language. This is because in this style of semantics only values can be associated to terms (even if the terms are ill typed). One could say that the rules of the big-step operational semantics are incomplete, since they do not specify how to associate a value to an application whose left-hand side has a value that is a numeric constant, or how to associate a value to an arithmetic operation where the value of one of the arguments is a term of the form `fun`, or a value to a conditional where the first argument has a value that is of the form `fun`. However, for well-typed terms the rules are complete. In other words, the three examples that we have just mentioned cannot arise.

We start by showing a *type-preservation-by-interpretation* lemma, which states that if a closed term t has type A then its value, if it exists, also has type A. This lemma corresponds to the subject reduction lemma of the small-step operational semantics.

Then we show, as for the small-step semantics, that a term of the form `fun` cannot have type `nat` and, similarly, that a numeric constant cannot have a type of the form A `->` B.

Since we know that the value of a term is either a number or a term of the form `fun`, we deduce that the value of a term of type `nat` is a numeric constant, and the value of a term of type A `->` B is a term of the form `fun`. Therefore, when interpreting a well-typed term, the left-hand side of an application will always be interpreted as a term of the form `fun`, the arguments of arithmetic operators will always be interpreted as numeric constants, and the first argument of an `ifz` will always be interpreted as a numeric constant.

Exercise 5.6 (Equivalent semantics) Show that the computation of a well-typed term produces a result under call by name small-step operational semantics if and only if it produces a result under call by name big-step operational semantics. Moreover, the result is the same in both cases. Show that the same property is true of the call by value semantics.

Does this result hold also for the untyped version of PCF? Hint: what is the result of `((fun x -> x) 1) 2`?

5.3 Denotational Semantics for Typed PCF

5.3.1 A Trivial Semantics

We mentioned above that one of the goals of functional languages is to shorten the distance between the notion of a program and the notion of a function. In other words, the goal is to bring the program closer to its denotational semantics.

We also said that it was difficult to give a denotational semantics for PCF without types, because functions did not have a domain of definition. Now that we have a type system for PCF, it is easier to give a denotational semantics.

We associate to each type a set

- $[\![\text{nat}]\!] = \mathbb{N}$,
- $[\![A \rightarrow B]\!] = [\![A]\!] \rightarrow [\![B]\!]$

and to each term t of type A an element $[\![t]\!]$ of $[\![A]\!]$. If the term t has free variables, we will associate meanings to these variables via a *semantic environment* e.

- $[\![x]\!]_e$ = a, if e includes the pair x = a,
- $[\![\text{fun } x{:}A \; \text{->} \; t]\!]_e$ = fun a:$[\![A]\!]$ -> $[\![t]\!]_{e,x=a}$,
- $[\![t \; u]\!]_e$ = $[\![t]\!]_e \; [\![u]\!]_e$,
- $[\![n]\!]_e$ = n,
- $[\![t \; + \; u]\!]_e$ = $[\![t]\!]_e$ + $[\![u]\!]_e$, $[\![t \; - \; u]\!]_e$ = $[\![t]\!]_e$ - $[\![u]\!]_e$,
  $[\![t \; * \; u]\!]_e$ = $[\![t]\!]_e$ * $[\![u]\!]_e$, $[\![t \; / \; u]\!]_e$ = $[\![t]\!]_e$ / $[\![u]\!]_e$,
- $[\![\text{ifz } t \; \text{then } u \; \text{else } v]\!]_e$ = $[\![u]\!]_e$ if $[\![t]\!]_e$ = 0 and $[\![v]\!]_e$ otherwise,
- $[\![\text{let } x{:}A \; = \; t \; \text{in } u]\!]_e$ = $[\![u]\!]_{e,x=[\![t]\!]_e}$.

This is really trivial: a program is a function and its semantics is the same function. Achieving this "triviality" is one of the goals in the design of functional languages.

Two remarks are in order. First, division by 0 produces an error in PCF, whereas it is not defined in Mathematics. To be precise, we should add a value error to each set $[\![A]\!]$ and adapt the definition given above. Second, in this definition we have forgotten the construction fix.

5.3.2 Termination

The only construct with a non-trivial denotational semantics is fix, because this construct is not usually found in everyday definitions of functions in Mathematics. Unlike PCF, mathematical definitions can only use fixed points of functions that do have a fixed point, and even then if there are several fixed points it is essential to specify which one we are taking. We left these issues aside when we defined PCF, it is now time to deal with them.

Consider a function that does not have a fixed point: the function fun x:nat -> x + 1. In PCF, we can build the term fix x:nat (x + 1). Similarly, the function fun f:(nat -> nat) -> fun x:nat -> (f x) + 1 does not have a fixed point but we can build the term fix f:(nat -> nat) fun x:nat -> (f x) + 1. On the other hand, the function fun x:nat -> x, has many fixed points, and still we can build the term fix x:nat x.

When we defined the operational semantics of PCF, we gave a reduction rule

$$\text{fix } x{:}A \; t \; \longrightarrow \; (\text{fix } x{:}A \; t/x)t$$

that explains the idea of a fixed point. Using this rule, we can see that the term a = fix x:nat (x + 1) reduces to a + 1, then to (a + 1) + 1, ... without ever reaching an irreducible term. Similarly, if g = fix f:(nat -> nat) fun x:nat -> (f x) + 1, the term g 0 can be reduced in two steps to (g 0) + 1 and then ((g 0) + 1) + 1, ... and again will never reach an irreducible term. The same thing happens with the term b = fix x:nat x, which reduces to b, and again to b, ... and will never reach an irreducible term. In other words, it appears that in PCF, when we take the fixed point of a function that does not have any, or that has more than one, the program does not terminate.

The situation is similar in Caml, where the program

```
let rec f x = (f x) + 1 in (f 0)
```

loops, or in Java with the program

```
class Loop {
  static int f (int x) {return f(x) + 1;}
  static public void main (String [ ] args) {
  System.out.println(f(0));}}
```

There are even functions, such as `fun x:nat -> x + x`, which have a unique fixed point but for which the `fix` construct in PCF produces a non-terminating computation: `fix x:nat (x + x)`.

In other words, to understand the denotational semantics of the fixed point operator, we need to understand first the semantics of terms that do not terminate.

The small-step operational semantics does not associate any result to these terms: there is no term V such that `fix x:nat (x + 1)` $\hookrightarrow$ V. And the big-step operational semantics does not give us more information. As we have already said, we could complete the relation $\hookrightarrow$ by adding a value $\bot$ such that `fix x:nat (x + 1)` $\hookrightarrow \bot$.

We have the same options in denotational semantics. We could define a partial function $[\![\ ]\!]$, and leave $[\![\text{fix x:nat } (x + 1)]\!]$ undefined, or we could add a value $\bot$ to $[\![\text{nat}]\!]$ and define $[\![\text{fix x:nat } (x + 1)]\!] = \bot$.

If we include the value $\bot$, the interpretation of a term of the form `t + u` will be obtained by interpreting first u and t, and if one of these terms loops, then the whole term `t + u` does. Thus, the denotational semantics of a term of the form `t + u` is defined as follows

- $[\![t + u]\!] = [\![t]\!] + [\![u]\!]$ if $[\![t]\!]$ and $[\![u]\!]$ are natural numbers,
- $[\![t + u]\!] = \bot$ if $[\![t]\!] = \bot$ or $[\![u]\!] = \bot$.

We can now remark that the function $[\![\text{fun x:nat } -> x + 1]\!]$, which did not have a fixed point when $\bot$ was not included, now has one: $\bot$. This value is precisely the one we will define as semantics for the term `fix x:nat (x + 1)`, which does not terminate. The function $[\![\text{fun x:nat } -> x]\!]$, which had several fixed points, now has an additional one $\bot$, and we will choose this one as semantics for the term `fix x:nat x`. The function $[\![\text{fun x:nat } -> x + x]\!]$, which had a unique fixed point 0 now has two: 0 and $\bot$, and again we will choose $\bot$ as semantics for the term `fix x:nat (x + x)` that does not terminate.

All the functions that we had mentioned have fixed points now, and if they have more than one, including $\bot$, we will choose the latter as our privileged value.

5.3.3 Scott's Ordering Relation

To make the ideas discussed above more precise, we define an ordering relation, called *Scott's ordering relation*, on the set $[\![\text{nat}]\!]$ as follows

and we define $[\![\texttt{fix x:nat t}]\!]$ as the least fixed point of the function $[\![\texttt{fun}$ $\texttt{x:nat -> t}]\!]$, forcing the use of the fixed point $\bot$ when more than one fixed point exist. It remains to prove that the least fixed point exists; we will use the fixed point theorem for this. To apply this theorem, we must show that the ordering relation that we defined on $[\![\texttt{nat}]\!]$ is weakly complete, and that the semantics of a program of type $\texttt{nat -> nat}$ is a continuous function.

More generally, we will build for each type $\texttt{A}$ a set $[\![\texttt{A}]\!]$ endowed with a weakly complete ordering relation, and we will show that the semantics of a program of type $\texttt{A -> B}$ is a continuous function from $[\![\texttt{A}]\!]$ to $[\![\texttt{B}]\!]$.

We start by defining the sets $[\![\texttt{A}]\!]$. The set $[\![\texttt{nat}]\!]$ will be defined as $\mathbb{N} \cup \{\bot\}$, with the ordering relation given above. The set $[\![\texttt{A -> B}]\!]$ is defined to be the set of all continuous functions from $[\![\texttt{A}]\!]$ to $[\![\texttt{B}]\!]$, with the ordering relation $\texttt{f} \leq \texttt{g}$ if for all $\texttt{x}$ in $[\![\texttt{A}]\!]$, $\texttt{f x} \leq \texttt{g x}$.

We can show that these ordering relations are weakly complete. The ordering on $[\![\texttt{nat}]\!]$ is weakly complete because any increasing sequence is either constant or has the form $\bot, \bot, \ldots, \bot, \texttt{n}, \texttt{n}, \ldots$ and in both cases there is a limit.

We will now show that if the ordering relations on $[\![\texttt{A}]\!]$ and $[\![\texttt{B}]\!]$ are weakly complete, then so is the ordering on $[\![\texttt{A -> B}]\!]$. Let us consider an increasing sequence $\texttt{f}_\texttt{n}$ over $[\![\texttt{A -> B}]\!]$. Using the definition of the ordering on $[\![\texttt{A -> B}]\!]$, for all $\texttt{x}$ in $[\![\texttt{A}]\!]$, the sequence $\texttt{f}_\texttt{n}$ $\texttt{x}$, whose values are in $[\![\texttt{B}]\!]$, is also increasing, and therefore has a limit. Let us call $\texttt{F}$ the function that associates to $\texttt{x}$ the element $\lim_\texttt{n}$ $(\texttt{f}_\texttt{n}$ $\texttt{x})$. We can show—but we will not do it here—that the function $\texttt{F}$ is in $[\![\texttt{A -> B}]\!]$, that is, it is a continuous function (this requires a lemma to permute limits). By construction, the function $\texttt{F}$ is greater than all the functions $\texttt{f}_\texttt{n}$, and it is the least such function. Therefore it is the limit of the sequence $\texttt{f}_\texttt{n}$. Any increasing sequence has a limit and the ordering relation on $[\![\texttt{A -> B}]\!]$ is therefore weakly complete.

Each set $[\![\texttt{A}]\!]$ has a least element, written $\bot_\texttt{A}$. The least element of $[\![\texttt{nat}]\!]$ is $\bot$, and the least element of $[\![\texttt{A -> B}]\!]$ is the constant function that returns the value $\bot_\texttt{B}$ for all arguments.

5.3.4 Semantics of Fixed Points

We can now go back to the denotational semantics of PCF, and add to the definition the missing case for $\texttt{fix}$

- $[\![\texttt{x}]\!]_\texttt{e} = \texttt{a}$, if $\texttt{e}$ contains the definition $\texttt{x} = \texttt{a}$,
- $[\![\texttt{fun x:A -> t}]\!]_\texttt{e} = \texttt{fun a}:[\![\texttt{A}]\!] \texttt{ -> } [\![\texttt{t}]\!]_{\texttt{e,x=a}}$,

- $[\![t\ u]\!]_e\ =\ [\![t]\!]_e\ [\![u]\!]_e$,
- $[\![n]\!]_e\ =\ n$,
- $[\![t\ \otimes\ u]\!]_e\ =\ [\![t]\!]_e\ \otimes\ [\![u]\!]_e$, if $[\![t]\!]_e$ and $[\![u]\!]_e$ are natural numbers, $\perp$ otherwise,
- $[\![\text{ifz } t \text{ then } u \text{ else } v]\!]_e\ =\ [\![u]\!]_e$ si $[\![t]\!]_e\ =\ 0$, $[\![v]\!]_e$ if $[\![t]\!]_e$ is a natural number different from 0 and $\perp_A$, where A is the type of this term, if $[\![t]\!]_e\ =\ \perp_{\text{nat}}$.
- $[\![\text{fix } x{:}A\ t]\!]_e\ =\ \text{FIX}\ (\text{fun } a{:}[\![A]\!]\ \text{->}\ [\![t]\!]_{e,x=a})$ where $\text{FIX}(f)$ is the least fixed point of the continuous function f,
- $[\![\text{let } x{:}A\ =\ t\ \text{in } u]\!]_e\ =\ [\![u]\!]_{e,x=[\![t]\!]_e}$.

To show that this definition is correct, we need to prove that if t is a term of type A then $[\![t]\!]$ is in $[\![A]\!]$, that is, we need to prove that the function is continuous. This is true, but we will not prove it here.

Exercise 5.7 What is the semantics of the term fun x:nat -> 0? And the semantics of fix x:nat x and (fun x:nat -> 0) (fix x:nat x)?

Exercise 5.8 What is the value of $[\![\text{ifz } t \text{ then } u \text{ else } v]\!]_e$, if $[\![t]\!]_e\ =\ 0$, $[\![u]\!]_e\ =\ 0$ and $[\![v]\!]_e\ =\ \perp_{\text{nat}}$?

We can now state the equivalence theorem for the two semantics. Let t be a closed term of type nat and n a natural number: $t\ \hookrightarrow\ n$ under call by name if and only if $[\![t]\!]\ =\ n$. The direct implication is not difficult to prove, but the converse is not trivial.

Exercise 5.9 Show, using the equivalence theorem, that if t is a closed term of type nat such that $[\![t]\!]\ =\ \perp$, there is no natural number n such that $t\ \hookrightarrow\ n$.

Exercise 5.10 Let G be the denotational semantics of the term fun f:(nat -> nat) -> fun n:nat -> ifz n then 1 else n * (f (n - 1)).

The denotational semantics of the term fix f:(nat -> nat) fun n:nat -> ifz n then 1 else n * (f (n - 1)) is the least fixed point of G. By the first fixed point theorem, this is the limit of the sequence $G^n(\perp_{\text{nat -> nat}})$. Which function is denoted by $\perp_{\text{nat -> nat}}$? And by $G^n(\perp_{\text{nat -> nat}})$? Identify the limit of this sequence.

Show that for any natural number p, there exists a natural number m such that $G^m(\perp_{\text{nat -> nat}})(p)\ =\ \lim_n G^n(\perp_{\text{nat -> nat}})(p)$.

Exercise 5.11 We consider the following elements in the set $[\![\text{nat -> nat}]\!]$: the function u that maps $\perp$ to $\perp$ and all other elements to 0, the function v_i that maps $\perp$ to $\perp$, i to 1 and all other elements to 0, and the function w_i that maps $\perp$ to $\perp$, 0, 1, ..., i-1 to 0 and all other elements to $\perp$.

Let F be an increasing function from $[\![\text{nat -> nat}]\!]$ to $[\![\text{nat}]\!]$, such that F u = 0 and for all i, F v_i = 1. Show that for all i, F w_i = $\perp$. Show that the function F is not continuous.

Show that it is not possible to write a PCF function that takes as argument a function g of type nat -> nat and returns 0 if for all n, g n = 0 and 1 otherwise.

Exercise 5.12 (An information-based approach to continuity) It might seem surprising that the notion of continuity is used to define the semantics of PCF, even though PCF works only with natural numbers, not with real numbers. In fact, the set of functions from $\mathbb{N}$ to $\mathbb{N}$, or the set of sequences of natural numbers, is very similar to the set of real numbers.

The intuition is that a real function f is continuous if to compute the initial n decimal places of f x it is sufficient to know a finite number of decimals in x. Unfortunately, this is technically false if x or f x are decimal numbers. We will say that a decimal number approximates a real number to the nth decimal place if the distance between the two is smaller than 10^{-n}. Thus, the number π has two approximations to the second decimal place: 3.14 and 3.15, and it makes sense to say that the function f is continuous if to compute a decimal approximation of f x to the nth place it is sufficient to have some decimal approximation of x.

The goal of this exercise is to show that, similarly, a function f from sequences of natural numbers to sequences of natural numbers is continuous if to compute the first n terms in f x it is sufficient to have an initial segment of x. If we agree to call a finite initial segment of the sequence a finite approximation, then we can rephrase it as follows: to compute an approximation of f x with n terms, it is sufficient to have a certain approximation of x.

Let u be a sequence of natural numbers, and let U be the element of $[\![\text{nat} \rightarrow \text{nat}]\!]$ that associates $\bot$ to $\bot$ and u_i to i.

Let V be a sequence with elements in $[\![\text{nat} \rightarrow \text{nat}]\!]$

$$[\bot \mapsto \bot, \ 0 \mapsto \bot, \ 1 \mapsto \bot, \ 2 \mapsto \bot, \ 3 \mapsto \bot, \ \ldots],$$
$$[\bot \mapsto \bot, \ 0 \mapsto u_0, \ 1 \mapsto \bot, \ 2 \mapsto \bot, \ 3 \mapsto \bot, \ \ldots],$$
$$[\bot \mapsto \bot, \ 0 \mapsto u_0, \ 1 \mapsto u_1, \ 2 \mapsto \bot, \ 3 \mapsto \bot, \ \ldots],$$
$$[\bot \mapsto \bot, \ 0 \mapsto u_0, \ 1 \mapsto u_1, \ 2 \mapsto u_2, \ 3 \mapsto \bot, \ \ldots],$$

$$\ldots$$

Show that the sequence V converges to U. Let F be a continuous function on $[\![\text{nat} \rightarrow \text{nat}]\!]$. Show that the sequence F V_i converges to F U. Show that the sequence F V_i p converges to F U p. Show that there exists a natural number k such that F V_k $p = F$ U p. Show that to compute F U p, it suffices to have the first k terms in U. Show that to compute the first n terms in F U it is sufficient to know a finite number of terms in U.

Consider the function that associates to a sequence u the number 0 if u is always 0, and 1 otherwise. Is this function continuous? Can it be written in PCF?

Finally, notice that in these two examples, the approximations—decimal numbers or finite sequences—contain a finite amount of information, whereas the objects that they approximate—real numbers or infinite sequences—contain an infinite amount of information.

Exercise 5.13 (Gödel's System T) To avoid non-terminating computations, we can replace `fix` by a `rec` construct to define functions by induction. All the programs in this language terminate, but the language is no longer Turing complete. Still, it is not easy to find a program that cannot be represented in this language, you need to be an expert logician to build such a program.

The function f defined by f 0 = a and f (n + 1) = g n (f n) is written rec a g. The small-step operational semantic rules for this construct are

$$\text{rec a g 0} \longrightarrow \text{a}$$

$$\text{rec a g n} \longrightarrow \text{g (n - 1) (rec a g (n - 1))}$$

if n is a natural number different from 0.

Program the factorial function in this language. Give typing rules for rec. Give a denotational semantics for this language.

Chapter 6
Type Inference

In many programming languages, for instance Java and C, programmers must declare a type for each of the variables used in the program, writing for example `fun x:nat -> x + 1`. However, if we know that + can only work with numbers, it is not difficult to show that in the term `fun x -> x + 1` the variable x has to be of type `nat`. We can then let the computer infer the types, rather than asking the programmer to write them. This is the goal of a *type inference* algorithm.

6.1 Inferring Monomorphic Types

6.1.1 Assigning Types to Untyped Terms

We will now use the original syntax of PCF, where variables are not explicitly typed. Instead of writing `fun x:nat -> x + 1`, we will write `fun x -> x + 1` as in Chap. 2.

We can now define the language of terms and the language of types independently. The language of terms in PCF is defined as in Chap. 2 and the language of types consists of

- a constant `nat`, and
- a symbol `->` with two arguments which does not bind any variable in its arguments.

```
A = X
  | nat
  | A -> A
```

As before, the relation $e \vdash t : A$ (read "the term t has type A in the environment e") can be defined by induction.

$$\frac{}{e \vdash x : A} \text{ if } e \text{ contains } x : A$$

G. Dowek, J.-J. Lévy, *Introduction to the Theory of Programming Languages*,
Undergraduate Topics in Computer Science,
DOI 10.1007/978-0-85729-076-2_6, © Springer-Verlag London Limited 2011

$$\frac{e \vdash u : A \quad e \vdash t : A \rightarrow B}{e \vdash t\ u : B}$$

$$\frac{(e,\ x : A) \vdash t : B}{e \vdash \text{fun}\ x \rightarrow t : A \rightarrow B}$$

$$\overline{e \vdash n : \text{nat}}$$

$$\frac{e \vdash u : \text{nat} \quad e \vdash t : \text{nat}}{e \vdash t \otimes u : \text{nat}}$$

$$\frac{e \vdash t : \text{nat} \quad e \vdash u : A \quad e \vdash v : A}{e \vdash \text{ifz}\ t\ \text{then}\ u\ \text{else}\ v : A}$$

$$\frac{(e,\ x : A) \vdash t : A}{e \vdash \text{fix}\ x\ t : A}$$

$$\frac{e \vdash t : A \quad (e,\ x : A) \vdash u : B}{e \vdash \text{let}\ x = t\ \text{in}\ u : B}$$

Some terms, for example the term fun x -> x, may have more than one type in this system. For instance, we can derive the judgement ⊢ fun x -> x : nat -> nat and also the judgement ⊢ fun x -> x : (nat -> nat) -> (nat -> nat). A closed term may have a type with free variables, for example the term fun x -> x has type X -> X in the empty environment.

We can prove that if a closed term t has a type A which contains variables in the empty environment, then t also has type θA for any substitution θ. For example, if we substitute the variable X by the type nat -> nat in X -> X, we obtain the type (nat -> nat) -> (nat -> nat) and this is one of the possible types for the term fun x -> x.

6.1.2 Hindley's Algorithm

We can now describe the type inference algorithm. We will first describe a version of the algorithm that has two phases. The first phase is similar to the type checking algorithm: it traverses the term, recursively, checking that the type constraints are satisfied, and computes the type of the term. There are however two important differences: first, when we are trying to type a term of the form fun x -> t in an environment e, since we do not know the type of the variable x we need to create a type variable X, extend the environment e with the declaration x : X, and type the term t in this extended environment. The second difference is that when typing an application t u, after computing types A and B for u and t, respectively, we cannot simply check that the type B has the form A -> C. Indeed, these two types might have variables. For this reason, at this point an equation between the types is generated B = A -> X. The second phase of the type inference algorithm solves these equations.

Let us illustrate the idea with an example: to type the term fun f -> 2 + (f 1) we must type the term 2 + (f 1) in the environment f : X. For this, we need to type the term 2, which has type nat, and the term f 1. The term 1 has type nat and the term f has type X. We generate the equation X = nat -> Y and the type of f 1 is Y. Once the terms 2 and f 1 are typed, we generate the equations nat = nat and Y = nat, and the type of the term 2 + (f 1) is nat. Finally, the type of the term fun f -> 2 + (f 1) is X -> nat and the equations that we need to solve are

$$X = \text{nat} \; \text{->} \; Y$$
$$\text{nat} = \text{nat}$$
$$Y = \text{nat}$$

This system of equations has a unique solution X = nat -> nat, Y = nat, and therefore the only type that we can assign to the term fun f -> 2 + (f 1) is (nat -> nat) -> nat.

We can describe the first part of the algorithm using a set of rules in the style of the big-step operational semantics (as we did for the type checking algorithm), but in this case the result of the interpretation of a term will not be a value or a type, it will be a pair of a type and a set of equations on types. We write e ⊢ t ⤳ A, E to denote the relation between the environment e, the term t, the type A and the set of equations E.

$$\frac{}{e \vdash x \rightsquigarrow A, \; \varnothing} \quad \text{if } e \text{ contains } x \; : \; A$$

$$\frac{e \vdash u \rightsquigarrow A, \; E \qquad e \vdash t \rightsquigarrow B, \; F}{e \vdash t \; u \rightsquigarrow X, \; E \cup F \cup \{B = A \; \text{->} \; X\}}$$

$$\frac{(e, \; x \; : \; X) \vdash t \rightsquigarrow A, \; E}{e \vdash \text{fun } x \; \text{->} \; t \rightsquigarrow (X \; \text{->} \; A), \; E}$$

$$\frac{}{e \vdash n \rightsquigarrow \text{nat}, \; \varnothing}$$

$$\frac{e \vdash u \rightsquigarrow A, \; E \qquad e \vdash t \rightsquigarrow B, \; F}{e \vdash t \otimes u \rightsquigarrow \text{nat}, \; E \cup F \cup \{A = \text{nat}, \; B = \text{nat}\}}$$

$$\frac{e \vdash t \rightsquigarrow A, \; E \qquad e \vdash u \rightsquigarrow B, \; F \qquad e \vdash v \rightsquigarrow C, \; G}{e \vdash \text{ifz } t \text{ then } u \text{ else } v \rightsquigarrow B, \; E \cup F \cup G \cup \{A = \text{nat}, \; B = C\}}$$

$$\frac{(e, \; x \; : \; X) \vdash t \rightsquigarrow A, \; E}{e \vdash \text{fix } x \; t \rightsquigarrow A, \; E \cup \{X = A\}}$$

$$\frac{e \vdash t \rightsquigarrow A, \; E \qquad (e, \; x \; : \; A) \vdash u \rightsquigarrow B, \; F}{e \vdash \text{let } x = t \text{ in } u \rightsquigarrow B, \; E \cup F}$$

In the application rule, the variable X is an arbitrary variable that does not occur in e, A, B, E and F. In the rules for fun and fix, it is an arbitrary variable that does not occur in e.

Let t be a closed term and let A and E be the type and the set of equations computed by this algorithm, that is, we have ⊢ t ⤳ A, E. A substitution σ = B_1/X_1, . . . , B_n/X_n is a *solution* of E if, for each equation C = D in E, the types σC and σD are identical. We can show that if a substitution σ is a solution of the set E, then the type σA is a type for t in the empty environment. In general, if e

⊢ t ⤳ A, E, then for any solution σ of E, σA is a type for t in the environment σe. Conversely, if A′ is a type for t in the empty environment, then there exists a substitution σ such that A′ = σA and σ is a solution of the set E of equations.

The second part of the algorithm deals with the type equations. The language of types does not have binders, it is a language generated by a constant nat and a symbol -> with two arguments. To solve the type equations, we use Robinson's unification algorithm, which solves equations in any arbitrary language without binders. This algorithm is in some respects similar to Gauss's algorithm to solve systems of equations. It proceeds by a series of transformations, defined as follows

- if an equation in the system is of the form A -> B = C -> D, it is replaced by the equations A = C and B = D,
- if an equation in the system is of the form nat = nat, it is removed from the system,
- if an equation in the system is of the form nat = A -> B or A -> B = nat, the algorithm fails,
- if an equation in the system is of the form X = X, it is removed from the system,
- if an equation in the system is of the form X = A or A = X, where X occurs in A and A is different from X, the algorithm fails,
- if an equation in the system is of the form X = A or A = X, where X does not occur in A and X occurs in other equations in the system, then X is substituted by A in all the other equations in the system.

This algorithm terminates, but the proof is not trivial. If the algorithm fails, then the system does not have a solution. If it terminates without failure, then the final system is of the form X_1 = A_1, ..., X_n = A_n, where the X_i are different variables and do not occur in the A_i. In this case, the substitution σ = A_1/X_1, ..., A_n/X_n is a solution of the initial system. We can prove that this substitution is a *principal* solution of this system, in other words, for any solution θ of the initial system, there is some substitution η such that $\theta = \eta \circ \sigma$. We write $\sigma = mgu(E)$—*most general unifier*: principal solution.

Let t be a closed term, and let A and E be such that ⊢ t ⤳ A, E. Let σ be a principal solution of E. Then the term t has type σA in the empty environment. Moreover, σA is a *principal* type of t, that is, for any other type B of t, there exists a substitution η such that B = $\eta\sigma$A.

6.1.3 Hindley's Algorithm with Immediate Resolution

There is a variant of Hindley's algorithm where instead of waiting until the end of the first phase to start solving the equations, the equations are solved as they are generated. In this case, instead of returning a type and a set of equations, the algorithm returns a type A and a substitution ρ that is a principal solution of the equations. We can also apply the substitution ρ to the type A as it is built.

The algorithm has the following property: if $e \vdash t \rightsquigarrow A, \rho$, then A is a principal type of t in the environment ρe. The algorithm is defined below.

$$\frac{}{e \vdash x \rightsquigarrow A, \varnothing} \quad \text{if e contains } x : A$$

$$\frac{e \vdash u \rightsquigarrow A, \rho \qquad \rho e \vdash t \rightsquigarrow B, \rho'}{e \vdash t u \rightsquigarrow \sigma X, \sigma \circ \rho' \circ \rho}$$

if $\sigma = \text{mgu}(B = \rho'A \rightarrow X)$

$$\frac{(e, x : X) \vdash t \rightsquigarrow A, \rho}{e \vdash \text{fun } x \rightarrow t \rightsquigarrow (\rho X \rightarrow A), \rho}$$

$$\frac{}{e \vdash n \rightsquigarrow \text{nat}, \varnothing}$$

$$\frac{e \vdash u \rightsquigarrow A, \rho \qquad \sigma \rho e \vdash t \rightsquigarrow B, \rho'}{e \vdash t \otimes u \rightsquigarrow \text{nat}, \sigma' \circ \rho' \circ \sigma \circ \rho}$$

if $\sigma = \text{mgu}(A = \text{nat})$ and $\sigma' = \text{mgu}(B = \text{nat})$

$$\frac{e \vdash t \rightsquigarrow A, \rho \qquad \sigma \rho e \vdash u \rightsquigarrow B, \rho' \qquad \rho' \sigma \rho e \vdash v \rightsquigarrow C, \rho''}{e \vdash \text{ifz } t \text{ then } u \text{ else } v \rightsquigarrow \sigma' C, \sigma' \circ \rho'' \circ \rho' \circ \sigma \circ \rho}$$

if $\sigma = \text{mgu}(A = \text{nat})$ and $\sigma' = \text{mgu}(\rho'' B = C)$

$$\frac{(e, x : X) \vdash t \rightsquigarrow A, \rho}{e \vdash \text{fix } x t \rightsquigarrow \sigma A, \sigma \circ \rho} \text{ if } \sigma = \text{mgu}(A = \rho X)$$

$$\frac{e \vdash t \rightsquigarrow A, \rho \qquad (\rho e, x : A) \vdash u \rightsquigarrow B, \rho'}{e \vdash \text{let } x = t \text{ in } u \rightsquigarrow B, \rho' \circ \rho}$$

Again, in the application rule X is an arbitrary variable that does not occur in e, A, B, ρ and ρ', and in the rules for fun and fix, it is a variable that does not occur in e.

Exercise 6.1 Give a principal type for the term fun x -> fun y -> (x (y + 1)) + 2. Describe all of its types.

Give a principal type for the term fun x -> x. Describe all of its types.

Exercise 6.2 (Unicity of principal types) A substitution σ is called a *renaming* if it is an injective map associating a variable to each variable. For example, the substitution y/x, z/y is a renaming. Let A be a type and σ, σ' two substitutions. Show that if $\sigma' \sigma A = A$ then $\sigma \mid_{FV(A)}$ is a renaming.

Deduce that if A and A' are two principal types of a term t then there exists a renaming θ, with domain $FV(A)$, such that $A' = \theta A$.

Exercise 6.3 In the general case of a language without binders, we can replace the first three rules in Robinson's unification algorithm by the two rules

– if an equation is of the form $f(u_1, \ldots, u_n) = f(v_1, \ldots, v_n)$, replace it by $u_1 = v_1, \ldots, u_n = v_n$,

 – if an equation is of the form $f(u_1, \ldots, u_n) = g(v_1, \ldots, v_p)$ where
   f and g are different symbols, fail.

In a language that consists of a symbol + with two arguments and integer constants, does the equation $(2 + (3 + X)) = (X + (Y + 2))$ have a solution? And the equation $X + 2 = 4$?

What is the difference between the equations in this language and the equations
over integers studied at high school?

Define the high school notion of solution using the small-step operational semantics of PCF. Does the equation $X + 2 = 4$ have a solution in this case?

6.2 Polymorphism

We have seen that the principal type of the term id = fun x -> x is X -> X.
This means that the term id has type A -> A for any type A. We could give it a
new type ∀X (X -> X) and add a rule so that if a term t has type ∀X A then
it has the type (B/X)A for any type B. A type language that includes a universal
quantifier is *polymorphic*.

In the system presented in the previous section, the term let id =
fun x -> x in id id was not typeable. Indeed, the typing rule for let requires that we type both fun x -> x and id id, but the latter is not typeable
because we cannot assign the same type to both occurrences of the variable id.
For this reason the term let id = fun x -> x in id id cannot be typed.
This could be seen as a flaw in the type system, because the term (fun x -> x)
(fun x -> x), obtained by replacing id by its definition, is typeable. Indeed,
to type this term it is sufficient to assign type nat -> nat to the first occurrence
of the bound variable x and type nat to the second.

If we give the type ∀X (X -> X) to the symbol id in the term let id =
fun x -> x in id id we can then use a different type for each occurrence of
id in the term id id, and the term becomes typeable.

Typing the term let id = fun x -> x in id id might seem a minor
issue, and adding quantifiers to the type language might seem a high price to pay
to obtain a marginal increase in power. However, this is a wrong impression. In
fact, in the extension of PCF with lists—see Exercise 3.14—, this feature allows
us to develop a unique sorting algorithm and apply it to all the lists, irrespective of
the type of their arguments: let sort = t in u. Polymorphism entails more
code reuse, and therefore more concise programs.

We will therefore give a quantified type to the variables bound in a let, but use
a standard type for variables that are bound in a fun or fix.

6.2.1 PCF with Polymorphic Types

We need to distinguish between types without quantifiers—we will continue to use
the word *types* for these—and quantified types, which we will call *type schemes*.

A scheme has the form $\forall X_1 \ldots \forall X_n \ A$ where A is a type. We will then define a language with two sorts: a sort for types and a sort for schemes. Since the sets of terms of each sort are disjoint in a many-sorted language, the set of types cannot be a subset of the set of schemes, and we will need to use a symbol [ ] to inject a type in the sort of the schemes. Thus, if A is a type, [A] will be the scheme consisting of the type A without any quantified variable.

The language of types and schemes is defined by

- a type constant nat,
- a type symbol -> with two type arguments, which does not bind any variable in its arguments,
- a scheme symbol [ ] with one type argument, which does not bind any variable in its argument,
- a scheme symbol $\forall$ with one scheme argument, which binds a variable in its argument.

```
A = X
  | nat
  | A -> A
S = Y
  | [A]
  | ∀X S
```

This language includes variables for every sort, in particular scheme variables. However, these variables will not be used.

An environment is now a list associating a scheme to each variable. We define inductively the relation "the term t has the scheme S in the environment e"

$$\frac{}{e \vdash x : S} \text{ if e contains } x : S$$

$$\frac{e \vdash u : [A] \quad e \vdash t : [A \to B]}{e \vdash t \ u : [B]}$$

$$\frac{(e, \ x : [A]) \vdash t : [B]}{e \vdash \text{fun } x \to t : [A \to B]}$$

$$\frac{}{e \vdash n : [\text{nat}]}$$

$$\frac{e \vdash u : [\text{nat}] \quad e \vdash t : [\text{nat}]}{e \vdash t \otimes u : [\text{nat}]}$$

$$\frac{e \vdash t : [\text{nat}] \quad e \vdash u : [A] \quad e \vdash v : [A]}{e \vdash \text{ifz } t \text{ then } u \text{ else } v : [A]}$$

$$\frac{(e, \ x : [A]) \vdash t : [A]}{e \vdash \text{fix } x \ t : [A]}$$

$$\frac{e \vdash t : S \quad (e, \ x : S) \vdash u : [B]}{e \vdash \text{let } x = t \text{ in } u : [B]}$$

$$\frac{e \vdash t : S}{e \vdash t : \forall X \ S} \text{ if X does not occur free in e}$$

$$\frac{e \vdash t \ : \ \forall X \ S}{e \vdash t \ : \ (A/X) S}$$

This inductive definition assigns a scheme to each term, in particular to variables. This is why variables are associated to schemes in the environment. However, when we type a term of the form `fun x -> t` or `fix x t`, we type `t` in an extended environment where the variable x is associated to a scheme `[A]` without quantifiers. A scheme can be associated to a term `t` only during the typing of a term of the form `let x = t in u`, and then this scheme is associated to the variable x.

To introduce quantifiers in the scheme associated to `t` we use the penultimate rule, which allows us to quantify a variable in the scheme `S` if the variable does not occur free in `e`. Thus, in the empty environment, after assigning the scheme `[X -> X]` to the term `fun x -> x` we can assign the scheme $\forall X$ `[X -> X]` to it. Note that in the environment `x : [X]`, after assigning the scheme `[X]` to the variable x we cannot assign the scheme $\forall X$ `[X]`.

Finally, note that if we have assigned a quantified scheme to a variable, or to an arbitrary term, we can remove the quantifier and substitute the free variable using the last rule. For example, in the environment `x : ∀X [X -> X]` we can assign the scheme `[nat -> nat]` to the variable x.

6.2.2 The Algorithm of Damas and Milner

We are now ready to define the inference algorithm. We will solve the equations on the fly, as we did in the second variant of Hindley's algorithm. The algorithm will be applied to a term `t` and an environment `e`, and it will return a type `A` and a substitution ρ such that the term `t` has the scheme `[A]` in the environment ρe. The only difference with respect to the second variant of Hindley's algorithm is in the first two rules

$$e \vdash x \ \leadsto \ (Y_1/X_1 \ \ldots \ Y_n/X_n) A, \varnothing$$

if `e` contains `x : ∀X_1 ... ∀X_n [A]` and $Y_1, \ldots, Y_n$ are new variables

$$\frac{e \vdash t \ \leadsto \ A, \rho \qquad (\rho e, \ x \ : \ \mathrm{Gen}(A, \rho e) \vdash u \ \leadsto \ B, \rho')}{e \vdash \mathtt{let} \ x \ = \ t \ \mathtt{in} \ u \ \leadsto \ B, \ \rho' \circ \rho}$$

where `Gen(A,e)` is the scheme obtained by quantifying in `[A]` all the type variables that are free in `[A]` but not in `e`.

We can prove that if `t` is a closed term, the type `A` computed by this algorithm is a principal type of `t`, that is, if $\vdash$ `t : [B]` then `B` is an instance of `A`.

Exercise 6.4 Consider the extension of PCF with a type symbol `list` with one argument, which is a type. We write `nat list` for the type of lists of natural numbers, `(nat -> nat) list` will be the type of lists of functions from natural numbers to natural numbers, and `(nat list) list` will be the type of lists where the elements are lists of natural numbers.

We add the following constructs to the language: a constant `nil` of type
`(A list)` for any type `A`, representing the empty list, `cons a l` of type
`(A list)` for any type `A` such that `a` has type `A` and `l` has type `A list`, which
will represent a list where the first element is `a` and `l` is the rest of the list, `ifnil`
`t then u else v` of type `A` if `t` has type `B list` and `u, v` are terms of type `A`,
to check whether the list `t` is empty or not, `hd l` of type `A` if `l` is of type `A list`,
that returns the first element of the list `l`, and `tl l` of type `A list` if `l` is of type
`A list`, that returns the list `l` without the first element. Write typing rules for this
extension of PCF. Write a type checker for this extension of PCF.

Program the function `map` that associates to a function `f` and a list t_1, ...,
t_n the list `f` t_1, ..., `f` t_n. What is the type of this function?

Program a sorting algorithm. What is the type of this algorithm?

In the type system described in this chapter, we can use quantified types for
variables that are bound in a `let`. We could try to give a quantified type to variables
that are bound in a `fun`. For example, we could give the type $\forall X \; (X \rightarrow X)$ to
the variable x in the term `fun x -> x x`, which will allow us to type this term.
The language obtained in this way is called System F, and was defined by Girard
and Reynolds. However, the typing relation is undecidable in System F, as shown
by Wells, and we cannot hope to have a type inference algorithm for System F.
Similarly, if we allow the variable bound by a `fix` to be polymorphic, the system
becomes undecidable, as shown by Kfoury. Restricting the polymorphic aspects of
the system to the `let` construct can be seen as a good compromise, it offers a good
level of code reuse and type inference.

Chapter 7
References and Assignment

Consider two numbers: π and the temperature in Paris. Today, the number π has a value between 3.14 and 3.15 and the temperature in Paris is between 16 and 17 degrees. Tomorrow, π will have the same value, but the temperature in Paris will probably change. In Mathematics, *numbers* are entities that do not change over time: the temperature in Paris is not a number that changes, it is a function that varies over time.

However, formalising the temperature of a system as a function of time is perhaps too general. It does not take into account the fact that the variation in temperature at a given point in time depends, in general, of the temperature at this point and not the temperature ten seconds earlier or ten seconds later. In general, a system does not have access to the full temperature function, just the current value of the function. This is why equations in Physics are generally differential equations and not arbitrary equations on functions.

In Computer Science, programs also use objects that vary over time. For example, in the program that manages the sale of tickets for a concert, the number of seats available varies over time: it decreases by one each time a ticket is sold. From the mathematical point of view, it is a function of time. However, to know whether it is possible or not to sell a ticket, or whether booking is no longer possible, the program only needs to know the current value of this function, not the full function: at a certain point t in time, it needs the value of the function at t.

For this reason, when we write such a program, we do not represent the number of places available for the concert as a function, that is, as a term of type nat -> nat—assuming a discrete clock—, which would mean that at each instant t we know the number of seats still available for the concert at each instant t'. This is clearly impossible, since it requires to know the number of seats available at each instant t' in the future. We cannot express this number by a term of type nat either, because as a number the value of a term of type nat in PCF cannot change over time. We have to introduce another sort of terms for the values that change over time: *references*, also called *variables* but we prefer not to use the word variable in this context, since the notion of a reference is very different from the notion of a variable in Mathematics and in functional languages.

G. Dowek, J.-J. Lévy, *Introduction to the Theory of Programming Languages*,
Undergraduate Topics in Computer Science,
DOI 10.1007/978-0-85729-076-2_7, © Springer-Verlag London Limited 2011

If x is a reference, we can do two things with it, get its current value !x and modify its value x := t, that is, contribute to the construction of the function that we mentioned above, asserting that the value of the function is now, and until further notice, the current value of the term t.

The issue of equality of "numbers that vary over time" is subtle. We could compare such a number, the temperature in Paris for instance, with a leaf in a tree: small, green and flexible in Spring, it becomes bigger, yellow and brittle in Autumn. There is clearly a change, but we know that it is the same leaf: nobody would believe that the little green leaf disintegrated and suddenly the big yellow leaf appeared *ex nihilo*. Although there is a transformation, the same leaf remains in the tree from March till October. This is an instance of the old paradox, that something can change while remaining the same. Similarly, the notion of temperature in Paris is always the same, even if the temperature changes over time. On the other hand, we can easily distinguish the temperature in Paris from the temperature in Rome: these are two different things, even if from time to time the temperature is the same in both cities.

One way to deal with this paradox is to consider the temperature in Paris and the temperature in Rome as functions: a function may take different values at two different points and remain the same function, and two different functions might take the same value at a given point.

In a program, if x and y are two references and we need to compare them, we should distinguish carefully between their equality as references, that is, whether x and y are the same thing or not—in mathematical terms: whether they are the same function of time—and equality of their contents, that is, whether the numbers !x and !y are the same at a particular point in time. In particular, equality of references implies that if we modify the value of x then the value of y also changes, but this is not the case if they are different references with the same value.

7.1 An Extension of PCF

We will now extend the language PCF with two new term constructors, written ! and :=.

The term x := 4 denotes an action: it updates the value associated to the reference x. Compare with the term fact 3, that we have already seen, and which also denotes an action: the computation of the factorial of 3. There is a difference between these two actions: the effect of the computation of the factorial of 3 is a value, whereas the effect of the action x := 4 is a change in the "global state" of the universe. Before this action, the reference x had, for instance, the value 0, and after this action it has the value 4. When we add references to PCF, the interpretation of a term is not just a value, but a value and a new state of the universe. This modification of the state is a *side effect* of the interpretation of a term.

The formal semantics of references in PCF defines the global state as a function from a finite set R to the set of values of PCF terms. The elements of the set R are called *references*. In the native programming language of a computer, its *machine language*, the set of references is fixed: it is the set of memory addresses of the computer. In other languages, the set R is arbitrary. In particular, when we define the semantics of a language, we do not distinguish between sets R and R' of the same cardinality (i.e., with the same number of elements). This means that programmers cannot know the exact set of memory addresses used to store the data.

In PCF, as well as in most programming languages, the values associated to references may change over time. Moreover, the set R itself may vary over time: it is possible to create a reference during the execution of the program. To do this, the language includes a construct ref. The side effect associated to the interpretation of the term ref t is the creation of a new reference whose initial value is the current value of the term t. The value computed by this interpretation is the reference itself.

Since the interpretation of the term ref t produces a value which is a reference, it is clear that references must be values in this extension of PCF.

7.2 Semantics of PCF with References

In the big-step operational semantics of this extension of PCF, the relation is of the form e, m ⊢ t ↪ V, m' where t is the term to be interpreted, e the environment where it will be interpreted, m the global state in which the interpretation will take place, V the value produced by the interpretation, and m' the new global state produced by the interpretation.

$$\frac{}{e,\ m \vdash x \hookrightarrow V,\ m} \quad \text{if e contains } x = V$$

$$\frac{e',\ m \vdash \text{fix } y\ t \hookrightarrow V,\ m'}{e,\ m \vdash x \hookrightarrow V,\ m'} \quad \begin{array}{l} \text{if e contains} \\ x = \langle \text{fix } y\ t,\ e' \rangle \end{array}$$

$$\frac{e,\ m \vdash u \hookrightarrow W,\ m'}{e,\ m' \vdash t \hookrightarrow \langle x,\ t',\ e' \rangle,\ m''} \\ \frac{(e',\ x = W),\ m'' \vdash t' \hookrightarrow V,\ m'''}{e,\ m \vdash t\ u \hookrightarrow V,\ m'''}$$

$$\frac{}{e,\ m \vdash \text{fun } x \to t \hookrightarrow \langle x,\ t,\ e \rangle,\ m}$$

$$\frac{}{e,\ m \vdash n \hookrightarrow n,\ m}$$

$$\frac{e,\ m \vdash u \hookrightarrow q,\ m' \qquad e,\ m' \vdash t \hookrightarrow p,\ m''}{e,\ m \vdash t \otimes u \hookrightarrow n,\ m''} \quad \text{if } p \otimes q = n$$

$$\frac{e,\ m \vdash t \hookrightarrow 0,\ m' \qquad e,\ m' \vdash u \hookrightarrow V,\ m''}{e,\ m \vdash \text{ifz } t \text{ then } u \text{ else } v \hookrightarrow V,\ m''}$$

$$\frac{e,\ m \vdash t \hookrightarrow n,\ m' \qquad e,\ m' \vdash v \hookrightarrow V,\ m''}{e,\ m \vdash \text{ifz } t \text{ then } u \text{ else } v \hookrightarrow V,\ m''} \qquad \text{if } n \text{ is a} \atop \text{number} \neq 0$$

$$\frac{(e,\ x = \langle \text{fix } x\ t,\ e \rangle),\ m \vdash t \hookrightarrow V,\ m'}{e,\ m \vdash \text{fix } x\ t \hookrightarrow V,\ m'}$$

$$\frac{e,\ m \vdash t \hookrightarrow W,\ m' \qquad (e,\ x = W),\ m' \vdash u \hookrightarrow V,\ m''}{e,\ m \vdash \text{let } x = t \text{ in } u \hookrightarrow V,\ m''}$$

We can now give rules for the three new constructs, ref, ! and :=

$$\frac{e,\ m \vdash t \hookrightarrow V,\ m'}{e,\ m \vdash \text{ref } t \hookrightarrow r,\ (m',\ r = V)}$$

if r is any reference not occurring in m'

$$\frac{e,\ m \vdash t \hookrightarrow r,\ m'}{e,\ m \vdash !t \hookrightarrow V,\ m'} \qquad \text{if } m' \text{ contains } r = V$$

$$\frac{e,\ m \vdash t \hookrightarrow r,\ m' \qquad e,\ m' \vdash u \hookrightarrow V,\ m''}{e,\ m \vdash t := u \hookrightarrow 0,\ (m'',\ r = V)}$$

The construction t; u whose semantics is obtained by interpreting t, throwing away the value obtained, then interpreting u, is not very interesting in a language without side effects, because in that case the value of the term t; u is always the same as the value of u, assuming t terminates. We can now add it to PCF

$$\frac{e,\ m \vdash t \hookrightarrow V,\ m' \qquad e,\ m' \vdash u \hookrightarrow W,\ m''}{e,\ m \vdash t;\ u \hookrightarrow W,\ m''}$$

We can also add now constructions while z, for, ... which were of no interest in a language without side effects.

Exercise 7.1 Write an interpreter for the language PCF with references.

The uncertainty that we mentioned at the beginning of the book regarding the evaluation of nested functions is finally elucidated.

Exercise 7.2 Consider the term

```
let n = ref 0
in let f = fun x -> fun y -> x
in let g = fun z -> (n := !n + z; !n)
in f (g 2) (g 7)
```

What is the value of this term? In which order will the arguments be interpreted in PCF? Why?

Modify the rules given above to obtain the value 2 instead of the value 9 for this term.

In Sect. 2.5 we remarked: "In the case of an application...". What do you think of this remark?

What is the value of this term in Caml?

Consider the following Java program

```
class Reference {
 static int n;
 static int f (int x, int y) {return x;}
 static int g (int z) {n = n + z; return n;}
 static public void main (String[ ] args) {
  n = 0; System.out.println(f(g(2),g(7)));}}
```

What is the value of this term?

In which order does Caml interpret its arguments? and Java?

Exercise 7.3 Is the value of the term

```
let x = ref 4 in let f = fun y -> y + !x
in (x := 5; f 6)
```

10 or 11? Compare with the answer for Exercise 2.8.

Exercise 7.4 Give the big-step operational semantics of the construction whilez. What is the value of the term given below?

```
let f = fun n ->
(let k = ref 1
 in let i = ref 1
 in (whilez (!i - n) do k := !k * !i;
     i := !i + 1 done; !k))
in f 3
```

Exercise 7.5 (The quirks of references under call by name) Consider the rules given above to define the big-step semantics of references. Do they follow a call by name or a call by value strategy? Give a similar rule for application under call by name, but keep the let in call by value. What is the value of the term let n = ref 0 in ((fun x -> x + x) (n := !n + 1; 4)); !n in call by value? And in call by name? What is the value of the term let n = ref 0 in ((fun x -> 2 * x) (n := !n + 1; 4)); !n in call by value? And in call by name?

Exercise 7.6 (Typing references) To type terms in the extension of PCF with references, we extend the language of types with a symbol ref, so that nat ref, for instance, is the type of references to a natural number. Thus, if t is a term of type A ref then !t is a term of type A.

Extend the typing rules given in Sect. 5.1 in order to type the language PCF with references.

Write a type-checking program for PCF with references.

The combination of references and polymorphism is subtle; we will not attempt to mix them in this exercise.

Exercise 7.7 (From imperative to functional programs) Consider a term t defining a function from natural numbers to natural numbers, with p arguments and a free variable n of type nat ref. We associate to this term a function with p + 1 arguments that returns a pair of natural numbers—see Exercise 3.13—such that the image of a_1, ..., a_p, m is the pair of natural numbers consisting of the value of the term let n = ref m in (t a_1 ... a_p) and the value of the term !n at the end of the interpretation. Which function will be associated to the term

– fun z -> (n := !n + z; !n)?

And to the term

– (fun z -> (n := !n + z; !n)) 7?

And to the term

– (fun x -> fun y -> x) ((fun z -> (n := !n + z; !n)) 2) ((fun z -> (n := !n + z; !n)) 7)?

Is it possible to program these functions in PCF without references?
   More generally,

– which function is associated to the term fun y_1 -> ... -> fun y_p -> 2?
– And to the term fun y_1 -> ... -> fun y_p -> y_1?
– And to the term fun y_1 -> ... -> fun y_p -> !n?
– If t is a term of type nat and f is the function associated to the term fun y_1 -> ... -> fun y_p -> t, which function is associated to fun y_1 -> ... -> fun y_p -> n := t?
– If t and u are terms of type nat, and f and g are the functions associated to the terms fun y_1 -> ... -> fun y_p -> t and fun y_1 -> ... -> fun y_p -> u, which function is associated to fun y_1 -> ... -> fun y_p -> (t + u)?
– If t and u are terms of type nat and f and g are the functions associated to the terms fun y_1 -> ... -> fun y_p -> t and fun y_1 -> ... -> fun y_p -> u, which function is associated to fun y_1 -> ... -> fun y_p -> (t; u)?
– If t is a term of type nat -> ... -> nat -> nat—with q arguments of type nat—u_1, ..., u_q are terms of type nat, and f, g_1, ..., g_q the functions associated to the terms fun y_1 -> ... -> fun y_p -> t and fun y_1 -> ... -> fun y_p -> u_1, ..., fun y_1 -> ... -> fun y_p -> u_q, which function is associated to fun y_1 -> ... -> fun y_p -> (t u_1 ... u_q)?

   Is it possible to program these functions in PCF without references?
   Write a program to transform a PCF term containing these symbols and a free variable of type nat ref into a program without it and with the same semantics.

Exercise 7.8 (For those who prefer to write x := x + 1 instead of x := !x + 1) Consider now a finite set of references, and let us extend PCF by introducing a constant for each of these references. These references will be called *mutable variables*. The symbol := applies now to a mutable variable and a term, written X := t.

If X is a mutable variable, the value that the operational semantics associates to the term X is the value associated to the reference X in the state available at the time of interpretation.

Give a big-step operational semantics for this extension of PCF.

Write an interpreter for this extension of PCF.

Exercise 7.9 (A minimal imperative language) Consider a language including integer constants, arithmetic operations, mutable variables—see Exercise 7.8—, assignment :=, sequence ;, a conditional ifz and a whilez loop (but without the usual notion of variable, fun, fix, let or application).

Give rules to define the operational semantics of this language. Write an interpreter for this language. Write a program to compute factorial in this language. What can we program in this language?

To conclude this chapter, we remark that in most programming languages there are two different ways to program the factorial function. For example, in Java, we can program it recursively

```
static int fact (int x) {
 if (x == 0) return 1; return x * (fact (x - 1));}
```

or iteratively

```
static int fact (int x) {
 int k = 1;
 for (int i = 1; i <= x; i = i + 1) k = k * i;
 return k;}
```

Should we prefer the first version or the second?

Of course, the theory of programming languages does not give us an answer to "moral" questions of the form "Should we...?" We could nevertheless say a few words about the way this question has evolved.

In the first programming languages—machine languages, assembly languages, Fortran, Basic, ...—only the second version could be programmed. Indeed, a program with loops and references is easier to execute in a machine that is itself, *in fine*, a physical system with a mutable state, than a program that requires evaluating a function defined via a fixed point.

Lisp was one of the first languages to promote the use of recursive definitions. With Lisp, for the first time, programs did away with references and side effects, and this simplified the semantics of the language, brought it close to mathematical language, allowed programmers to reason over programs in an easier way, and facilitated the task of writing complex programs. For example, it is much easier to write a program to compute the derivative of an algebraic expression using recursion than keeping track of a stack of expressions that are waiting to be treated. It was then natural to contrast the pure functional style of programming with the "impure" imperative one.

But the first implementations of functional languages were very slow in comparison with those of imperative languages, precisely because, as we have said, it is more difficult to execute a functional program on a machine, which is a physical system, than it is to execute an imperative program. During the 1990's, the compilation techniques for functional languages made such a huge progress that efficiency is no longer a valid argument against functional programming today, except in the domain of intensive computation.

Moreover, all modern languages include both functional and imperative features, which means that today the only valid argument to justify the choice of a particular style should be its simplicity and ease of use.

From this point of view, it is clear that not all problems are identical. A program that computes derivatives for functional expressions is easier to express in functional style. In contrast, when we program the Logo turtle it is more natural to talk about the position of the turtle, its orientation, . . . —that is, its state at a given instant. It is also natural to talk about the actions that the turtle does: to move, to write a line, . . . , and it is not easy to express all this in a functional way: in fact, it is not natural to think of the turtle's actions as functions over the space of drawings.

There is still one point that remains mysterious: programs, whether functional or imperative, are always functions from inputs to outputs. If imperative programming brought us new ways of defining functions, which in certain cases are more practical from a Computer Science point of view than the mathematical definitions that are typical of functional languages, we could wonder whether they would also be more practical for mathematicians. However, so far the mathematical language has not adopted the notion of reference.

Chapter 8
Records and Objects

8.1 Records

In the equations describing the movement of two bodies that exert a force on each other, for example, a star and a planet, their positions are represented by three coordinates (functions of time). This leads to a system of differential equations with six variables. However, instead of "flattening" them, we can group them in two packages of three variables each, obtaining a system of differential equations with vector variables. There are mathematical tools to pack several values into one: the notion of a pair, which can be iterated to build tuples, and the notion of a finite sequence.

In programming languages we also need tools to pack several values into one. The tools that we have for this are the notion of a *pair*, the notion of an *array*, the notion of a *record*, the notion of an *object* and the notion of a *module*. The components of those structures are called *fields*.

8.1.1 Labelled Fields

To represent the position of an object on Earth by latitude, longitude and altitude, we can use a tuple with three components: the first one is the latitude of the object, the second its longitude and the third its altitude. If we decide that the tuple (a,b,c) is the pair $(a,(b,c))$, then the element in the left-hand side is the latitude, the one in the left-hand side of the right-hand side component is its longitude and the one on the right of the right-hand side component is its altitude. There are several other combinations, and our choice here is clearly arbitrary.

If instead we decide that the tuple (a,b,c) is represented by a function from $\{0,1,2\}$ to $\mathbb{R}$ that associates a to 0, b to 1 and c to 2, then the latitude of the object is the real number associated by this function to 0, its longitude is the number associated to 1 and its altitude is the number associated to 2. Again, there are other alternatives, and our choice is arbitrary.

G. Dowek, J.-J. Lévy, *Introduction to the Theory of Programming Languages*,
Undergraduate Topics in Computer Science,
DOI 10.1007/978-0-85729-076-2_8, © Springer-Verlag London Limited 2011

There is no reason to place these values in a specific position in the tuple, or to associate them with one number rather than another. Moreover, if in a program we need to change the data structure to add another field, we will have to update the program in several places. These modifications are likely to introduce errors, and we might end up confusing longitude and temperature...

Since it is more convenient for programmers to identify the fields by using a name—"latitude", "longitude", ...—instead of a position or a number, programming languages offer this possibility. This leads us to a notion of tuple with labelled fields, called *record*. From a mathematical point of view, a record is a function whose domain is an arbitrary finite set (rather than an initial segment of $\mathbb{N}$), and the elements of the set are the *labels* of the record.

The idea of referring to the fields by a name instead of using their position in the tuple can also be used in the context of a function call. In some experimental languages, instead of writing `f(4,2)` we write `f(abscissa = 4, ordinate = 2)` or equivalently `f(ordinate = 2, abscissa = 4)`.

8.1.2 An Extension of PCF with Records

To extend PCF with records, we add three symbols to the language: a symbol `{}` to build records, a symbol `.` to access a field in a record, and a symbol `<-` to build a new record identical to one previously constructed except for the value of one field.

Before introducing these symbols we need to introduce a new sort for labels and an infinite set of constants, one for each label. Notice that there is no symbol to bind a variable of sort label, therefore there will be no such variables in a closed term. Moreover, the language does not include any other symbol to build terms of sort `label`, just the constants. Therefore, in a closed term the only subterms of sort `label` are constants. We can then add to PCF

- a symbol `{}` with $2n$ arguments that does not bind any variables; the arguments at odd positions are labels and the ones at even positions are terms,
- a symbol `.` with two arguments, where the first is a term and the second a label, which does not bind any variable,
- a symbol `<-` with three arguments where the first is a term, the second a label and the third a term, which does not bind any variable.

Exercise 8.1 In the definition of language that we gave in Chap. 1, each symbol has a fixed number of arguments. We cannot have then a symbol like `{}` which could have for instance 6 or 8 arguments. How could we fix the definition given above to make it compatible with the notion of language defined in Chap. 1? Hint: What is a list?

The term `{}(`$l_1,t_1,$ `...,` l_n,t_n`)` will be written `{`l_1 `=` $t_1,$ `...,` l_n `=` t_n`}`, the term `.(t,l)` will be written `t.l` and the term `<-(t,l,u)` will be written `t(l <- u)`.

The small-step operational semantics of PCF will now include the following rules

$$\{l_1 = t_1, \ldots, l_n = t_n\}.l_i \longrightarrow t_i$$

$$\{l_1 = t_1, \ldots, l_n = t_n\}(l_i <\!\!- u) \longrightarrow$$

$$\{l_1 = t_1, \ldots, l_{i-1} = t_{i-1}, l_i = u,$$

$$l_{i+1} = t_{i+1}, \ldots, l_n = t_n\}$$

Similarly, the big-step operational semantics is extended with the following rules

$$\frac{t_1 \hookrightarrow V_1 \cdots t_n \hookrightarrow V_n}{\{l_1 = t_1, \ldots, l_n = t_n\} \hookrightarrow \{l_1 = V_1, \ldots, l_n = V_n\}}$$

$$\frac{t \hookrightarrow \{l_1 = V_1, \ldots, l_n = V_n\}}{t.l_i \hookrightarrow V_i}$$

$$\frac{t \hookrightarrow \{l_1 = V_1, \ldots, l_n = V_n\} \quad u \hookrightarrow W}{t(l_i <\!\!- u) \hookrightarrow \{l_1 = V_1, \ldots, l_{i-1} = V_{i-1}, l_i = W,}$$
$$l_{i+1} = V_{i+1}, \ldots, l_n = V_n\}$$

Notice that in these rules the terms of sort `label` are not interpreted. This is because, as mentioned above, these terms are constants.

Exercise 8.2 Write an interpreter for PCF with records.

Exercise 8.3 The goal of this exercise is to represent a Logo turtle with a record containing an abscissa, an ordinate, and an angle. The turtle should have an internal state so that it can move without changing its identity—see the introduction to Chap. 7. There are two alternatives: the turtle can be defined as a record of references to real numbers, or as a reference to a record of real numbers. Write the function `move-forward` in both cases.

In this exercise we assume that there is a type of real numbers and all the necessary operations.

In the big-step operational semantics that we gave for PCF with records, the interpretation of the term $\{a = 3 + 4, b = 2\}$ requires to perform the addition of 3 and 4. In contrast, once the value $\{a = 7, b = 2\}$ is built, an access to the field a does not require to perform an arithmetic operation.

An alternative would be to delay the addition and assume that the term $\{a = 3 + 4, b = 2\}$ is a value that can be interpreted as itself. In this case, we will need to interpret the term $3 + 4$ each time there is an access to the field a. We could say that this semantics is a *call by name* one, as opposed to the semantics we gave above, which follows the *call by value* strategy.

In call by name, the rules of the operational semantics are

$$\overline{\{l_1 = t_1, \ldots, l_n = t_n\} \hookrightarrow \{l_1 = t_1, \ldots, l_n = t_n\}}$$

$$\frac{t \hookrightarrow \{l_1 = t_1, \ldots, l_n = t_n\} \quad t_i \hookrightarrow V}{t.l_i \hookrightarrow V}$$

$$\frac{t \hookrightarrow \{l_1 = t_1, \ldots, l_n = t_n\}}{t(l_i <- u) \hookrightarrow \{l_1 = t_1, \ldots, l_{i-1} = t_{i-1}, l_i = u, \\ l_{i+1} = t_{i+1}, \ldots, l_n = t_n\}}$$

Exercise 8.4 Write an interpreter for PCF with records following the call by name semantics.

If we compare these two semantics of records, we are lead to make the same comments as for the semantics of functions in call by value vs. call by name: the interpretation of `let x = {a = fact 10, b = 4}` in `x.b` requires the computation of the factorial of 10 in call by value, but not in call by name. On the other hand, the interpretation of `let x = {a = fact 10, b = 4}` in `x.a + x.a` under call by name triggers twice the computation of the factorial 10. The interpretation of `let x = {a = fix y y, b = 4}` in `x.b` produces an infinite loop under call by value, whereas it successfully returns 4 under call by name. Finally, when we also have references, the side effects of the interpretation of a field could be repeated several times if we access the filed several times—see Exercise 7.5.

For example, if we build a record x with a field a that is a reference to a natural number, initially 0, and a function inc that increases this number by one, and then we write a term that increases this value and returns it, we obtain

```
let x = {a = ref 0}
in let inc = fun y -> (y.a := 1 + !(y.a))
in (inc x; !(x.a))
```

Under call by value, this term produces the result 1, as one expects. However, a call by name interpretation will access three times the field a of the record x, that is, it will interpret three times the term `ref 0`, creating three references that point to the value 0. The third reference, created by the interpretation of the term `!(x.a)`, is never updated and therefore the interpretation of the programme above under call by name produces the result 0.

To make sure that the call by value and the call by name interpretations produce the same result, we should avoid side effects—such as the creation of a reference in the example above—during the interpretation of fields. We can rewrite the term as follows

```
let r = ref 0
in let x = {a = r}
in let inc = fun y -> (y.a := 1 + !(y.a))
in (inc x; !(x.a))
```

which guarantees that the value will be 1, whether in call by value or call by name.

Exercise 8.5 (Types for records) Consider a type `person` for records with three fields: `surname`, `name` and `telephone`. Show that we can program the three functions x(surname <- y), x(name <- y) and x(telephone <- y) without using the symbol <-, which means that this symbol is superfluous.

Will this symbol be still superfluous if we have a type contactable including all the records which contain at least the field telephone?

If we have a type person and a type contactable, do we still have unicity of types?

8.2 Objects

Programs usually deal with various kinds of data, often structured as records. For example, a company's computer system might deal with order forms from customers, invoices, pay slips.... A customer order might be represented as a record including the identification of the object ordered, the quantity requested... To print the data there are several alternatives. We could write a unique function print that starts by checking which kind of data we want to print—order form, pay slip...—and then prints it in a different format depending on the kind of data. Or we could write several functions: print_order_form, print_pay_slip... Alternatively, we could define a record print where each field is a printing function. Yet another option would be to make each printing function a part of the type. Such a data type is called a class, and its elements are called *objects*.

In the most radical object-oriented programming style, each object, for instance, each order form, includes a different function print. An order form is then a record that contains, in addition to the standard fields—identification of the item requested, number of items ordered, ...—a field print defining the printing function that should be used to print the object.

Some languages, for instance Java, associate a print function to each class rather than each object. Thus, all the objects in the class share the printing function—whether static or dynamic. If we do not want to share the printing function for two objects t and u in the same class C, we need to define two sub-classes T and U of C, which inherit all the fields of C but redefine print differently.

8.2.1 Methods and Functional Fields

An object is simply a record where some fields are functions. In Java, where functions are not first-class objects, we must distinguish the fields that are functions from those that are not; the functional ones are called *methods*.

In a language where functions are first-class objects, like PCF, this distinction is not necessary. Objects are then simply records, and we can program in an object-oriented style in the extension of PCF with records defined previously in this chapter.

Exercise 8.6 The program that manages the sale of tickets for a concert is an object with the following fields

- a reference to a natural number: the number of orchestra seats available,
- a reference to a natural number: the number of balcony seats available,
- a function that takes an object and a natural number as arguments—0 for orchestra and 1 for balcony—and returns the number 0 or the number 1 to indicate whether the booking is closed or there are still seats in that area,
- a function that takes an object and a natural number as arguments—0 for orchestra and 1 for balcony—, and reserves a seat by decreasing the number of seats available in that area; by convention it returns the value 0.

Program this object in PCF with records.

Typing systems for records and objects are out of the scope of this book. We will only say that if we give type A to the object defined in Exercise 8.6, then A must be the Cartesian product of nat ref, nat ref, A -> nat -> nat and A -> nat -> nat. We cannot define the type A as (nat ref) × (nat ref) × (A -> nat -> nat) × (A -> nat -> nat), because this is a circular definition. To define this type, we need to introduce a fixed point operator on types.

If X -> Y denotes the space of functions from X to Y and B is a set with at least two elements, then the recursive equation A = (A -> B) does not have a solution. Indeed, it follows from Cantor's theorem that the cardinal of the set A -> B is strictly greater than that of A. The equation A = (nat ref) × (nat ref) × (A -> nat -> nat) × (A -> nat -> nat) does not have a solution either. As with the construction fix in PCF, it is not trivial to give a denotational semantics for the fixed point operator on types.

8.2.2 What Is "Self"?

If t is the object built in Exercise 8.6, to know whether the booking is closed or there are still orchestra tickets, we need to interpret the term t.free t 0. Indeed, the function t.free takes an object u and a natural number n and indicates whether the field associated to n in u—orchestra if n = 0, balcony if n = 1—is zero or not. In other words, the method free is *static*, as defined for example in Java.

We now want the method free of the object t to apply to the object t itself, that is, we want to invoke it by interpreting the term t#free 0 instead of t.free t 0. In other words, we want this method to be *dynamic*.

One way to achieve this is to consider the term t#l as an abbreviation for t.l t. The difficulty here is that if t is an object and l a label in this object, we can only use the term t#l if the field l is a function of type A -> ... where A is the type of t itself. In other words, we can only use the term t#l if l is the label of a method. If l is the label of a field that is not a method, we still need to write t.l.

To avoid this distinction, we can state that all fields are functions. If a field a of an object t has the value 3, we transform it into a field with functional value fun

$s \rightarrow 3$. Thus, the term $t\#a$, that is, $t.a$ t or $(fun \ s \ \rightarrow \ 3) \ t$, is interpreted as the value 3.

The first argument of each method in the object is then a bound variable, which is usually called $self$ or $this$. In fact, most programming languages use a special variable $self$ or $this$ which is implicitly bound in the object, and which denotes the object itself.

When all methods in a record are terms of the form $fun \ x \ \rightarrow \ ...$, they can be interpreted as themselves, and we can simplify the rule

$$\frac{fun \ x_1 \ \rightarrow \ t_1 \ \hookrightarrow \ V_1 \ ...}{\{l_1 \ = \ fun \ x_1 \ \rightarrow \ t_1, \ ...\} \ \hookrightarrow \ \{l_1 \ = \ V_1, \ ...\}}$$

by using

$$\{l_1 \ = \ fun \ x_1 \ \rightarrow \ t_1, \ ...\} \ \hookrightarrow \ \{l_1 \ = \ fun \ x_1 \ \rightarrow \ t_1, \ ...\}$$

Similarly, the rule

$$\frac{t \ \hookrightarrow \ \{l_1 \ = \ V_1, \ ...\}}{t.l_i \ \hookrightarrow \ V_i}$$

specialises to

$$\frac{t \ \hookrightarrow \ \{l_1 \ = \ fun \ x_1 \ \rightarrow \ t_1, \ ...\}}{t.l_i \ \hookrightarrow \ fun \ x_i \ \rightarrow \ t_i}$$

and finally the rule

$$\frac{t \ \hookrightarrow \ \{l_1 \ = \ V_1, \ ...\} \qquad u \ \hookrightarrow \ W}{t(l_i \ \texttt{<-u} \ ) \ \hookrightarrow \ \{l_1 \ = \ V_1, \ ..., \ l_i \ = \ W, \ ...\}}$$

can be replaced by

$$\frac{t \ \hookrightarrow \ \{l_1 \ = \ fun \ x_1 \ \rightarrow \ t_1, \ ...\}}{t(l_i \ \texttt{<-} \ (fun \ y \ \rightarrow \ v)) \ \hookrightarrow}$$
$$\{l_1 \ = \ fun \ x_1 \ \rightarrow \ t_1, \ ..., \ l_i \ = \ (fun \ y \ \rightarrow \ v), \ ...\}$$

To force all fields to be functions, we can modify the language of records, passing from a record language to an object-oriented language. The symbol $\{\}$ now binds a variable in each even argument—terms—, the symbol $.$ is replaced by the symbol $\#$, the symbol $\texttt{<-}$ now binds a variable in the third argument.

The term $\{\} (l_1, \ s_1 \ t_1, \ ..., \ l_n, \ s_n \ t_n)$ is written $\{l_1 \ = \ \varsigma s_1 \ t_1, \ ..., \ l_n \ = \ \varsigma s_n \ t_n\}$, the term $\# (t,l)$ is written $t\#l$ and the term $\texttt{<-}(t,l, s \ u)$ is written $t(l \ \texttt{<-} \ \varsigma s \ u)$. The rules of the big-step operational semantics are now

$$\frac{}{\{l_1 \ = \ \varsigma s_1 \ t_1, \ ..., l_n \ = \ \varsigma s_n \ t_n\} \ \hookrightarrow}$$
$$\{l_1 \ = \ \varsigma s_1 \ t_1, \ ..., l_n \ = \ \varsigma s_n \ t_n\}$$

$$\frac{t \ \hookrightarrow \ \{l_1 \ = \ \varsigma s_1 t_1, \ ..., \ l_n \ = \ \varsigma s_n t_n\} \qquad (t/s_i) t_i \ \hookrightarrow \ V}{t\#l_i \ \hookrightarrow \ V}$$

$$\frac{t \ \hookrightarrow \ \{l_1 \ = \ \varsigma s_1 t_1, \ ...\}}{t(l_i \ \texttt{<-} \ \varsigma s \ u) \ \hookrightarrow \ \{l_1 \ = \ \varsigma s_1 t_1, \ ..., \ l_{i-1} \ = \ \varsigma s_{i-1} \ t_{i-1},}$$
$$l_i \ = \ \varsigma s \ u, \ l_{i+1} \ = \ \varsigma s_{i+1} t_{i+1}, \ ...\}$$

Exercise 8.7 Write an interpreter for the language PCF with objects.

Exercise 8.8 (Late binding) Consider the term

```
(({x = ςs 4, f = ςs fun y -> y + s#x} (x <- ςs 5))#f) 6
```

Is the value of this term 10 or 11? Compare this result with that of Exercise 2.8.

8.2.3 Objects and References

The standard definition of object includes a notion of internal state, which evolves in time. Thus, it combines the notion of object and reference, which are clearly separate in the definition of functional object given above.

In a language with objects and references, when a non-functional field a = u is transformed into a = fun x -> u, the interpretation of fun x -> u does not produce the side effects produced by the interpretation of u. It is only when we access the field that the side effects will be visible. Thus, the behaviour is similar to that of records under call by name. The term

```
let x = {a = fun s -> ref 0}
in let inc = fun s -> (s#a := 1 + !(s#a))
in (inc x; !(x#a))
```

is interpreted as the value 0 and not 1 as the term

```
let x = {a = ref 0}
in let inc = fun s -> (s.a := 1 + !(s.a))
in (inc x; !(x.a))
```

in call by value. We need to rewrite this term as follows

```
let r = ref 0
in let x = {a = fun s -> r}
in let inc = fun s -> (s#a := 1 + !(s#a))
in (inc x; !(x#a))
```

if we want the interpretation to be the value 1.

Exercise 8.9 When we interpret a term of the form t#1, how many times is the term t interpreted? If the interpretation of t includes side effects, how many times will they take place? How can we force the term t to be interpreted only once?

Chapter 9
Epilogue

The first goal of this book was to present the main tools to define the semantics of a programming language: small-step operational semantics, big-step operational semantics, and denotational semantics.

We have stressed the fact that these three tools have the same purpose. In the three cases, the goal is to define a relation $\hookrightarrow$ between a program, an input value and an output value. Since the goal is to define a relation, the question that arises naturally is: how do we define relations in mathematical language?

The answer is the same in the three cases: the means to achieve the goal is the fixed point theorem. However, the similarity is superficial, because the fixed point theorems are used in different ways in the three semantics. By giving rise to inductive definitions, and hence reflexive-transitive closures, the fixed point theorem plays a major rôle in operational semantics. In contrast, it plays a minor rôle in denotational semantics, because it is only used to give the meaning of the construction `fix`. The denotational semantics of a language without fixed point, such as Gödel's System T—see Exercise 5.13—can be defined without using the fixed point theorem.

To highlight the differences, we can look at the rôle of derivations. To establish that a term `t` has the value `V` in operational semantics, it is sufficient to show a derivation, or a sequence of reductions, that is, finite objects. In contrast, in denotational semantics the meaning of a term of the form `fix` is given as the least fixed point of a function, that is, a limit. For this reason, to establish that the value of a term `t` is `V` we sometimes need to compute the limit of a sequence, that is, we sometimes need to deal with an infinite object.

Operational semantics have an advantage over denotational ones, because the relation $\hookrightarrow$ can be defined in a more concrete way operationally. But on the other hand, operationally we can only define relations that are recursively enumerable, whereas denotationally we can define arbitrary relations. For this reason, in operational semantics we cannot complete the definition of the relation $\hookrightarrow$ by adding a value $\bot$ for the terms that do not terminate, because the resulting relation is not recursive, it cannot be effectively defined by induction. In contrast, denotationally it is not a problem to add such a value.

G. Dowek, J.-J. Lévy, *Introduction to the Theory of Programming Languages*,
Undergraduate Topics in Computer Science,
DOI 10.1007/978-0-85729-076-2_9, © Springer-Verlag London Limited 2011

We see here the dilemma that arises from the undecidability of the halting problem: we cannot complete the relation $\hookrightarrow$ by adding $\perp$ for the non-terminating terms, and at the same time define it inductively. We have to choose between completing the relation or defining it inductively, which leads to two different semantics. The readers who have followed logic courses before will recognise here the same issues that distinguish the truth judgements that are inductively defined, by the existence of a proof, from those that are defined by their validity in a model.

The second goal of this book was to give the semantics of some programming language features: explicit definitions of functions, functions defined by fixed points, assignment, records, objects. . . . Here again, since the goal is to define functions, it is useful to start by looking at the ways in which functions are defined in Mathematics. In general, the comparison between the mathematical language and programming languages is fruitful, since the mathematical language is the closest we have to programming languages. This comparison shows some common points, but also some differences.

The purpose of the study of programming language features is not to be exhaustive, but to show some informative examples. The point to remember is that, in the same way that Zoology is not the study of all the animal species one after the other, the study of programming languages should not consist of studying all languages one after the other. They should be organised according to their main features.

We could continue this study by defining data types and exceptions. The study of data types would give us the opportunity to use again the fixed point theorem, and Robinson's unification algorithm, of which matching is a particular case. Going forward in this direction we could study the notion of backtracking which leads to Prolog. Other important points that we have left aside are the polymorphic typing of references, the notion of array, imperative objects, modules, type systems for records and objects (and in particular the notion of sub-type), concurrency. . . .

The final goal of this book was to present a number of applications of these tools, in particular for the design and implementation of interpreters and compilers, and also the implementation of type inference systems. The main point here is that the structure of a compiler is derived directly from the operational semantics of the language to be compiled. The next step would be the study of implementation techniques for abstract machines, and this would lead us to the study of memory management and garbage collection. We could also study program analysis, and design systems to deduce in an automatic or interactive way properties of programs, for instance, the property that states that the value returned by a sorting algorithm is a sorted list.

The last point that remains to discuss is the rôle of the theory of programming languages, and in particular whether its purpose is to describe the existing programming languages, or to propose new languages.

Astronomers study the galaxies that exist, and do not build new ones, whereas chemists study the existing molecules and build new ones. We know that in the latter case, the order in which theories and production techniques appear may vary: the transformation of mass into energy was achieved long time after the theory of relativity, whereas the steam engine appeared before the principles of thermodynamics were established.

The theory of programming languages has enabled the development of new features, such as static binding, type inference, polymorphic types, garbage collection, ... which are now available in commercial languages. In contrast, other functionalities, such as assignments and objects, were introduced in programming languages wildly, and the theory has been slow to follow. The development of a formal semantics for these constructs led in turn to new proposals, such as the recent extensions of Java with polymorphic types.

The theory of programming languages has neither an exclusively descriptive rôle nor an exclusively leading rôle. It is this going backwards and forwards between the description of existing features and the design of new ones that gives the theory of programming languages its dynamics.

References

1. Abadi, M., Cardelli, L.: A Theory of Objects. Springer, Berlin (1998)
2. Dybvig, R.K.: The Scheme Programming Language, 2nd edn. Prentice Hall, New York (1996). www.scheme.com/tspl2d/
3. Gunter, C.A.: Semantics of Programming Languages: Structures and Techniques. MIT Press, Cambridge (1992)
4. Kahn, G.: Natural semantics. In: Proceedings of the Symp. on Theoretical Aspects of Computer Science, TACS, Passau (1987)
5. Mitchell, J.C.: Foundations for Programming Languages. MIT Press, Cambridge (1996)
6. Mitchell, J.C.: Concepts in Programming Languages. Cambridge University Press, Cambridge (2002)
7. Peyton Jones, S., Lester, D.: Types and Programming Languages. Prentice Hall, New York (1992)
8. Pierce, B.C.: Types and Programming Languages. MIT Press, Cambridge (2002)
9. Plotkin, G.D.: LCF considered as a programming language. Theor. Comput. Sci. **5**, 223–255 (1977)
10. Plotkin, G.D.: A structural approach to operational semantics. Technical Report DAIMI FN–19, Computer Science Department, Aarhus University, Aarhus, Denmark, September 1981
11. Reynolds, J.C.: Theories of Programming Languages. Cambridge University Press, Cambridge (1998)
12. Scott, D.: Continuous Lattices. Lecture Notes in Math., vol. 274, pp. 97–136. Springer, Berlin (1972)
13. Weis, P., Leroy, X.: Le langage Caml, 2nd edn. Dunod, Paris (1999)
14. Winskel, G.: The Formal Semantics of Programming Languages. MIT Press, Cambridge (1993)

G. Dowek, J.-J. Lévy, *Introduction to the Theory of Programming Languages*,
Undergraduate Topics in Computer Science,
DOI 10.1007/978-0-85729-076-2, © Springer-Verlag London Limited 2011

Index

G. Dowek, J.-J. Lévy, *Introduction to the Theory of Programming Languages*,
Undergraduate Topics in Computer Science,
DOI 10.1007/978-0-85729-076-2, © Springer-Verlag London Limited 2011